Foundations of Free Will

OTHER WORKS
BY ROBERT BOLTON

The Order of the Ages:
(*World History in the Light of a Universal Cosmogony*)

Keys of Gnosis

Self and Spirit

The One and the Many

Person, Soul, and Identity

Robert Bolton

Foundations
of
Free Will

ANGELICO PRESS
SOPHIA PERENNIS

First published in the USA,
Sophia Perennis, 2010
Angelico Press/Sophia Perennis edition, 2024
© Robert Bolton

Series editor: James R. Wetmore

For information, address:
Angelico Press,
169 Monitor St.
Brooklyn, NY 11222
angelicopress.com

ISBN 978-1-59731-099-4 (pbk)
ISBN 978-1-59731-241-7 (hbk)

Cover design: Michael Schrauzer

CONTENTS

Preface 1

Introduction 2

Sources for the Idea—Relevance of Platonism—Aristotelian Principles—Neoplatonic and Christian Ideas—The Modern Situation

1 Plato and the Possibility of Free Will 14

Early Ideas of Causality—The Two Rival Powers—Modes of Necessity—A Human and Cosmic Order—Reason the Key to Freedom—The Two Ways

2 Plotinus and the Essence of Freedom 35

The Neoplatonic Background—Doubts about Free Will—A Source of Free Will—Freedom's Causality—Choosing the Choice—The Basis of Choice: the "Conjoint"—Pure Intellect and Human Intellect

3 Alexander and the Denial of Necessity 60

An Opponent of Stoicism—Uncaused Events—Causality, Sequence and Coincidence—The Reality of Non-Being—Motivation in Broken Series—What is Fate?

4 The Three Grounds of Freedom Compared 82

Plato's Freedom and Necessity—Plotinian Freedom—The Augustinian Perspective—"Ascending and "Descending" Volition—Legal Functions of Free Will—Deliberation and Assent—The Necessity of Freedom

5 Moral Responsibility: For and Against 105

Questions of Practical Importance—Some Opposing Arguments—Three Natures in Man—The Unity of the Person—Diverse Causes of Passions—Kant's Response to Hume—Ruled by One's Own Law—Limits to the Imperative

6 Some Modern Free Will Arguments 127

Real Minds, Real Agents—Determinism is Incoherent—Why Predictions Fail—No Free Will, No Intelligence—The Bifurcation of Nature—The Excess of Causes—Reversal of Entropy—Soul as a Power of Self-motion

Conclusion 149

The Limits of Causality—Mind as Cause—The Foundation of Values—Freedom for Self-Realization—True and False Freedom

Appendix: Kant and Free Will 163

A Kantian Ambivalence—Causal Selection—Kant's Account of Causality—One-Sidedly Traditional—Moral Law from Free Will—Causal Origination—A Rational Idea of Happiness

Index 185

Preface

The need to justify a belief in free will is always present and relevant because no other idea has so many implications for the conduct of life, and because there are always so many experiences which appear to cast doubt on it. Even the simple alternatives of either believing in it or not have verifiable effects on behavior, although any advantages resulting from a belief in free will do not amount to a valid argument for it. If it is real, it must in any case operate in a world where many things can be shown to be determined according to causal laws, and for this reason, arguments for free will must be such as not to compromise or invalidate causality.

Although arguments for free will are supportive and necessary from a religious point of view, I have not made much reference to theological accounts of this subject and its relation to God. This is not because I do not understand their importance, but because I am concerned only to show how belief in free will is rational in itself, whereas in the larger context of religion the question of pragmatic reasons for it could easily intrude. Besides that, there is the further complication that religions are mostly ambivalent about free will, while some even deny it. This is because, where human freedom is related to God, it must be seen as a created thing, that is to say, caused by God, even though not necessarily subject to anything else.

Theologically, therefore, free will is both a cause and an effect at the same time, which is perfectly valid, but that nevertheless distracts attention from the most essential issue treated here, namely that of whether it should exist at all. It is assumed that the self-creative potential of our freedom, if real, is not creation in a literal sense, but is rather the basis on which created beings realize their most important possibilities. From the ideas about free will offered here, its role in religion and in life in general should be apparent.

Introduction

Sources for the Idea

The plan of this study is to base the reasoning on what some leading philosophers have thought concerning the freedom of the will, these being principally Plato, Plotinus, and Alexander of Aphrodisias, giving full attention to their arguments for it. At the same time, further arguments, and arguments based on theirs, will be introduced wherever possible in support of this idea in what follows. A very long timespan is covered by the authorities quoted, not so as to introduce a greater variety of content, but because the perennial nature of the free will problem creates affinities between philosophers who are otherwise far apart in every sense.

The line of reasoning drawn from my sources will tend against the idea of a homogeneous or monistic reality, which is necessarily the basis of determinism. Where dualism appears in the writings of the philosophers cited here, I shall not attempt to construct any alternative to it, therefore. The question of mind-body interaction will necessarily arise, but the treatment of it will not be on Cartesian lines, but rather on Platonic. The latter doctrine emphasizes the concreteness of soul or mind, and minimizes that of material things, in defiance of common sense ideas. This would help solve the problem as to how an abstract mind could operate on things supposedly more concrete than itself, and would also employ a traditional idea of material concreteness which is similar to that of modern physics.

My method also follows that of Proclus in his *Providence and Fate*, where the idea of a determined world order is also fully accepted, with freedom consequently being something superadded to it, from a human point of view, while being ultimately essential to it. The pursuit of this idea makes the determined order of nature actually necessary as the ground of freedom, rather than a negating force competing with it, however much their representations may conflict in human minds. Necessity will be represented as relating to free will as the earth with its fixed shape and cardinal points relates to the direction-finding of a traveler.

This projected complementarism between these two realities will be used to support the view that, while free will is latent in all mankind, there is no end to the different degrees to which it can be actualized. The philosophers studied here have ideas which can be joined to a traditional view of man, according to which he is situated on a dividing-line between two realms, those of nature, where necessity rules, and of the spirit, where freedom rules. By this means, some objective basis will be sought for the experience of moral conflict.

The absence of free will in nature will be regarded as all of a piece with its absence in the collective human order as well. No freedom is envisaged in the interactions of nations or any other of man's institutions, and no increase in our knowledge of them makes them seem any less bound by fixed laws. But the same does not seem to apply to the human individual, however, whence we may suppose that if free will is to be found at all, it is to be found in persons. For everything besides the human individual, that is, all natural and collective domains, capture and defense of territory, self-sustenance, and self-propagation, are not only the dominant activities, but are effectively the only ones possible, no matter whether they appear in more or less refined forms.

This does not mean, however, that freedom will be treated as though it were in a wholly different world from that of natural forces. Instead, more attention will be paid to the common sense idea of free will's being able to effect real changes in the world of causality, without, for all that, being the same as a natural cause itself. This will involve an account of natural processes which will make at least some of them susceptible to causal energies of radically different kinds. The world so envisaged will not be homogeneous, either in its causal series or in the metaphysical status of the beings which interact in it.

In this way, the tendency of the study will be as inclusive as possible, allowing for both determination and freedom, and a connecting principle between them, subject to our understanding, and by means of which we can adjust our relations to both of them. Rather than trying to explain away any of the major elements of human experience, it will be a question of trying to discover an integrated system embracing very diverse realities, so as to avoid tendencies to force the world into some limiting system which would explain only by mutilating what was to be explained.

Relevance of Platonism

As the aim is to validate individual free will on the basis of what some philosophers have said in this connection, it will not be possible to ensure that a balanced treatment of their work as a whole can be given. Where Plato is concerned, there is very little direct reference to the will or free will, but much which pertains to it *a priori* in some of his works. That he does believe in free will is in any case evident from what he says about crime and punishment in his *Laws*, where it is even referred to as such. Plato gives a vision of a world made from a mingling of profoundly differing realities, either of which man is able to identify himself with to some degree.

Nevertheless, one may hold a firm implicit belief in free will, along with other beliefs of a more scientific kind, while doing little to work out the connection between them. This appears to be true of Plato, who can be seen to have a reason-centered idea of free will, like that of Kant. They are notably agreed in not seeing freedom in caprice or in liberty of indifference, but rather in a union of the will with truth. They both also share a markedly dualistic tendency, which I shall follow in a modified form in this study. My ideas in this regard are not affected by the question as to whether the mind-matter dualism actually does account for everything, or whether, as Spinoza thought, there are innumerable other, equally different principles, which we ignore simply because they do not enter into our makeup. Rather, it should be a question of two real and distinct principles with which we are intimately involved, one of which contains inherently the condition for the understanding of the other, and of the relation between them.

Much use will be made of Plato's theory in the *Timaeus*, for the purpose of establishing a conception of the Platonic idea of free will, assimilated to rationality and opposed to necessity. The extent to which reliance is placed on this theory may raise the question as to whether detailed use of it would require a more literal understanding of it than would be warranted by the cosmogonic myth it is understood to be today. However, Plato himself warns us against taking the details of this dialogue too literally, as he more than once specifically calls it simply "a probable account", but at the same time there are many theoretical points made by means of the myth which may reasonably be believed, once it is seen that they are a kind of shorthand for abstract argument.

Thus a commitment to the theory does not require us to believe that the Demiurge literally took a strip of material to make into the World Soul, whereas we may believe that a creative power has formed a psychic substance qualified according to harmonic ratios, to be the most essential reality of the universe. Similarly, there is no need to believe that human souls were taken from a mixing bowl containing the residue of this substance, for us to be able to believe that man is formed psychically by analogy with this psychic principle of the universe. As long as we bear in mind the distinction between the mythical details and the points made by means of them, we shall be able to see the theoretical grounds for Plato's conception of man's fundamental choice between intelligible and material realities, which for him formed the ultimate purpose of freedom.

The most essential argument in this context, however, underlying even these theoretical views about man and the universe as conveyed by the myth, is the famous Platonic inversion of the order of reality between the materially concrete and the universals which inform it. Plato does not argue for this directly as a rule, but rather proceeds on the presupposition that the psychic and noetic reality is in some sense primordial relative to the natural world, with the assumption that the results of theorizing on this basis will give an insight into the nature of things, and that this objective nature will retrospectively confirm the implications of this conception. Proof has to begin somewhere, and to ask more than this could come close to asking for proof that proof existed.

Aristotelian Principles

The next two philosophers both derive from Plato, though in quite different ways. One of them, Plotinus, is a Platonist in both form and intention, though one who has learned from Aristotle where metaphysics is concerned. The other is Alexander of Aphrodisias, who is a follower of Aristotle, and the most important commentator on him in his time (early 3rd century AD) The choice of two such different philosophers after Plato results from a deep division in Plato's thought where free will is concerned. On the one hand, he has an otherworldly metaphysical idea of it, while in his *Laws* he maintains it in a strictly practical and legalistic form, and it is never made clear how these two conceptions are related. Consequently, the Neoplatonists concentrated almost wholly on Plato's metaphysic of freedom, while Aristotle and his followers are chiefly concerned with the legalistic aspect, and when they do consider the metaphysical one, it is not in terms of Plato's metaphysics.

The reason for my choice of a follower of Aristotle, like Alexander, and not Aristotle himself, is owing primarily to the fact that Alexander is the author of a book *On Fate,* which is directly relevant to the present subject, besides which, his account of Aristotle's thought was always accepted as authoritative. Only by the inclusion of both Plotinus and Alexander can one give a full development of what was implicit in Plato. Despite the title of his book (which in modern terms means determinism), Alexander is strongly committed to free will, so much so that he has been accused of denying some of the reality which was understood to be fate-governed in any case. For him, fate was little more than a set of ideal patterns which nature strove to realize, but without any necessity. Although he taught free will, and lived in the 3rd century AD., he was not a Christian. His belief in free will was wholly due to his conclusion that it was the most logical interpretation of Aristotle's thought relating to the subject.

There is a marked influence from Aristotle's *Nichomachean Ethics,* and from Plato's *Laws.* His main intention is to vindicate the common sense conviction that we are free and are masters of our actions, in a way which would be supportive of society's system of rewards and punishments. Freedom is therefore considered almost entirely on the plane of action, as one would expect from a common sense orientation, but ironically, the defense of such a position leads Alexander into the highly metaphysical question of there being events which have no causes. He seeks support for this idea from Aristotle's *Metaphysics,* while extending the meaning of what is said there. With only one exception, he never draws on Plato's metaphysical ideas in regard to freedom.

At the same time, he is drawn further into metaphysical realms with the need to introduce the idea of an uncaused First Cause, and thence to the idea of uncaused causes in general. These ideas will be related to modern thought, where the question of uncaused events also arises. Relationships will also be indicated between the ideas of Alexander and Kant in regard to reason as a basis for free will, as indeed it is for Plato as well. Some of the issues in regard to freedom discussed by Alexander are far from being settled at the present time, and have been through periodic revivals. From the Platonic point of view, Alexander's view of free will is an instructive example of how far a certain aspect of Plato's thought can be taken. For all the metaphysics, the practical implications remain uppermost, as is shown by their relation to the legal need to distinguish between voluntary and involuntary offences. The common sense conviction as to this distinction is not challenged, so it is more a question of making the theory fit the facts as we find them, in this instance and in Alexander's treatment of the subject as a whole.

Neoplatonic and Christian Ideas

In contrast to this is the manner in which Plotinus analyses free will. He also makes explicit an idea of free will which was simply latent in Plato, and in this case it defies common sense ideas almost as much as does the Platonic idea of the real and the unreal. Taking his point of departure from Plato's assimilation between freedom (as the opposite of Necessity), and rationality, Plotinus equates the fullest degree of it with a state of contemplation upon which no particular choices are incumbent. The common sense idea of freedom is not actually denied, but is confined to being only a diluted or compromised form of the above.

Such thinking is characteristic of the otherworldliness that was entering into the leading forms of thought in the 3rd century AD, since the denial of full freedom to the life containing the maximum of practical choices only makes sense, or at least, most easily makes sense, on the assumption that this is not man's true life, but rather a preparation for another. At this time there was in fact a broad agreement between Christian teachings and those of the later Platonists in this regard. Unfortunately, otherworldly doctrines, which should build a vision of higher possibilities on the foundation of natural life, can easily become deformed into mere substitutes for the life to which they should give deeper meaning. Then one is liable to get the worst of both worlds, namely an actual world which is incurably bad, and a true world which has no intelligible connection with it. There was an early tendency in this direction, which was led by some schools of Gnosticism, and Plotinus opposed them in much the same way as orthodox Christianity attempted to do. This unity of tendency is also to be seen from the fact that the Plotinian deduction from Plato, that the acme of freedom lay in the contemplative rather than in the active life, was to be a decisive influence on St.Augustine, and thence on the Western Christian tradition.

This point of view was enshrined in a Pythagorean parable quoted by Cicero, according to which mankind is divided into three classes, comparable with those who go to the games; the first, and lowest class, are those who go to compete; the second and middling class are those who go so as to sell things to the spectators; and the third and highest class, are those who go only to watch the spectacle. Such was the scale of priorities which remained unchallenged among the educated through the millennia.

Only in modern times has this evaluation been reversed, and that more for social and economic reasons than because of any new and profounder insight. (Contemplative man is not a good consumer.) The traditional idea has become generally misunderstood in any case, since the operative factor is not so much a contemplative life lived with a robotic exclusiveness, as the ideal based on it which serves as a moral compass-bearing amid the conflicting choices of life.

The Neoplatonic departure from the usual idea of freedom has also the effect of helping us solve an age-old problem as to why man should be as free to do evil as to do good, in a world which is believed to be made by a benign Creator. At the price of some common sense evaluations, we should be able on this basis to see how true freedom is primarily a freedom for good, whereas a freedom for evil is rather a *chimaera* produced by the uncritical assumption of a symmetry between good and evil which is formally Manichaean, and is inconsistent with anything but systematic pessimism. While there can of course be no evil without some degree of freedom, it is by no means of the same order as that of its positive form, as I wish to show in what follows.

Another way in which the free will argued for here differs from the form it wears in most religious contexts will appear in that it will not be presumed to be fully present in everyone equally, but rather a possibility which develops out of an originally unfree state. At the same time, it will be opposed to scientifically-based denials of it, which are apt to be based on studies of persons who are either sick or subnormal, these being the types that psychological science is determined by.[1]

I argue for it as a possibility, wherever my commentary on the philosophers will allow, which by understanding and application can be made into an increasingly experienced reality. In this way I do not have to refute either scientific necessity in its own sphere, or for that matter, the traditional idea of it according to which mankind as a whole is borne along by a tide of determination or fate, which Christianity adopted in its own terms, those of the Fall.

In Neoplatonic and Christian teachings this was always a subject closely connected with salvation. Individual liberation from fate was inculcated, though this was never expected to alter the world's fate-bound course, no matter how great the change in the individual. As

---

1. This position of philosophy in relation to religion and science is well expressed by J. Needleman in the conclusion to *The Heart of Philosophy*, in regard to free will.

the less familiar of the two forms of the doctrine, the ideas of Iamblichus for the Neoplatonic position are worthy of note in this regard:

> The soul that descends to us from the worlds follows the periods of the worlds; but that which is intelligibly present from the intelligible transcends the genesiurgic motion, and through this, *a liberation from fate,*[2] and the ascent to the intelligible Gods, are effected. . . .[3]

According to Iamblichus, therefore, each soul has elements drawn from the cosmic cycle to which it belongs, while it also possesses some share in an essence superior to the cosmos. Its freedom lies in its ability to give first place to the latter.

The Modern Situation

But while the necessity for the freedom of the will is clear enough for the purposes of mainstream religious faith, it is equally true that there are sound humanistic reasons for affirming it, as well. Experience shows that, without a belief in free will, most human beings will not bother to develop their natural capacities to the full. A major enemy of this vitalizing belief is the bureaucratic control of society, which instills by its very presence a constant subliminal message to everyone that everything will be much the same, no matter what we do or fail to do individually. This adversely affects the general will to live, which in turn multiplies the more extreme cases where this goes as far as nihilism, usually expressed in cravings for means to oblivion.

There is also a connection between modern trends against belief in free will, and a widespread discrediting of the dualistic theory of knowledge, in favor of a more or less monistic point of view of the self in the world. Far from being a matter for epistemology, this theory has strong psychological and cultural overtones. The subject-object conception is suggestive of a position of centrality and

2. My emphasis.
3. Iamblichus, *The Mysteries*, sec. VIII, chaps. vi and vii, Thomas Taylor, tr. See also R. Bolton, *Keys of Gnosis*, chap. 9.

mastery, and of many possibilities of action, which a single subject view of the self can never give, which is a further reason why I shall not try to argue against dualism where it appears in the texts I shall examine. Such considerations cannot be offered as a way of establishing the reality of the subject-object relation, since they assume it, but they do imply that this relation expresses some deep reality in our nature. It should therefore be retained short of overwhelming evidence to the contrary, such as does not yet appear to have been manifested.

My treatment of the thought of Plato, Plotinus, and Alexander will thus run counter to a trend which has advanced unchecked for a long time, but which may now be reaching the limits of its expansion. Much of the impetus behind it comes from as far back as the deterministic philosophy which grew out of the advances of 17th Century science, and the times when the classical conception of physics was the only one. There is inevitably a long time lag between the rise of new theoretical insights and the changes they make to society as a whole, so that deterministic points of view would no doubt survive for a long time after their basis was undermined by further advances. Even though such developments directly concern only a quite small number of persons, the fact remains that what prevails on the intellectual high ground has an impact on the culture far out of proportion to the numbers of those involved, for good or ill.

There have been reactions in defense of the classical determinist position, of course, but the motivation behind them is not really philosophical, but springs rather from social and historical causes. For centuries there was an almost mandatory belief in free will and moral responsibility which was applied crudely and undiscriminatingly, with the result that innumerable persons were judged to be morally guilty for faults which were really owing only to natural defects and not to a bad will. Such imbalances always end with reactions which go too far in the opposite direction, in this case, taking the form of a determination to deny the reality of free will, even where its reality is clearly a relevant question. Although a certain class of injustices is removed in this way, a new one is created at the same time, as where people are not adequately protected from crime by a society which is officially committed to seeing good in everyone, excepting only those who do not see good in everyone. The promotion of social equality is closely bound up with this, because equality implicitly means non-responsibility, and therefore no free will, and because it is moral differences which are most liable to make individuals unequal.

However, the issues of free will are by no means confined to morality and moral responsibility, because they also determine the cultural vitality of civilization. The choice of creative endeavours in artistic, spiritual and scientific realms is necessarily affected by the prevailing beliefs about the range of activities possible in human life. When these possibilities are believed to be diminished, it is the higher forms of culture which are hit hardest, rather as though the lower ones came from a lower part of the psyche which was less sensitive to the influences of ideas. Consequently, the Conclusion will attempt to join the ideas of the philosophers considered here to other and more general issues from both philosophy and science which are congenial to the idea of the individual person as a center of independent causality, not only for moral purposes, but so as to give some theoretical support for the idea of man as a creative being.

A general remark may be timely here in regard to the role of argument relating to a subject like free will, because free will is a subject which can be placed in the general category of forms of human behavior. Everything in this category is liable to come under the "self-fulfilling prophecy" principle, according to which the pursuit of any consistent line of action will of itself invoke and connect with the supportive evidence the theory behind it needs. But if theories in this category can elicit the required responses from both oneself and others without necessarily being objectively true, this would seem to seriously weaken any arguments put forward for them.

However, it can be argued against this that free will does also belong in a unique category, in which this normally weak kind of argument is in fact strong. This is because the possibility of the "self-fulfilling" principle implies a flexibility in the workings of the natural world, by which it can be made to partially correspond with different conceptions. But it is precisely this flexibility in the way in which a certain region of natural law operates under the combined action of mind and will which is a precondition for there being a real free will which is effectual in the world. For this reason, self-verification will not only not weaken the arguments, but will rather support them in this case, while it would not do so in any other.

1

Plato and the Possibility of Free Will

Early Ideas of Causality

The discussion of Plato's relation to free will shall be based mainly on what he says in the *Timaeus,* which is concerned with natural science and the constitution of man. There is much in this dialogue which is a detailed development of an important argument in the *Philebus,*[1] where it is shown that the various elements which compose man physically are all taken from the universe, which possesses them in unlimited quantity. As the duality of body and soul is accepted, this premise leads to the conclusion that the soul also, and its faculties and its wisdom, are likewise taken from the universe, since there is no other possible source. Thus it could be said that even the most spiritual things about us are more ancient than we, and pre-exist us in the universe. The secret of the will's choice will be found in man's own constitution.

Plato, like Kant, had a conception of the unknowable which could only be reached by a kind of quasi-knowledge at best, but Kant confined it to the transcendental realm, whereas Plato saw it in the substratum of nature, where matter is dominant. The mere fact that the material world is in a state of constant change, is enough to rule out there being knowledge of it, rather than opinion. Such is the origin of Plato's low opinion of the reality of the material world, which does not encourage anyone to see it as a system of necessary laws, though what Plato calls Necessity (*ananke*) is repeatedly said to exist in it. This Necessity will be seen to be conceived more like

---

1. See *Philebus,* 29b–30d.

that of the arbitrary will of a tyrant, than that of regular order, although that is not excluded.

Thus Necessity has a meaning in the *Timaeus* which differs from the modern scientific idea of it. It was taken to refer to all events that came about through physical causes without purpose or mutual relevance, and without the assumption that all events are equally rigorously determined. Plato's thought in this regard is influenced by that of his own age, as manifest by the thought of Thucydides, as Cornford has pointed out. Their common idea of nature allowed that the intervention of human agency was possible within it because the natural course of events was in any case often broken in upon by other natural forces. Physical necessity may often bring about conditions which for us are mere chance, and are opposed to our purposes.

> Thucydides sees the field of human action divided between human *foresight* and *chance*; Plato sees the world of physical events divided between *divine purpose* and *chance associated with necessity*.[2]

This reflects a pre-scientific view of nature, but it cannot be disposed of simply on that basis, because the scientific view is so largely dependent on artificially controlled conditions. The scientific view of nature gets support from the impact on life of many technical devices, each of which reproduces the ideal conditions of the laboratory in its own way. If technology went so far as to create a wholly controlled environment, the older view would seem to be completely falsified, but even this would not be logically applicable to nature as it is in itself, which was what Plato was concerned with.

We do not find direct references to free will in Plato's works, however, which can give rise to misunderstandings. It has even been denied that Plato has any idea of free will at all:

> [V]olition, as an independent faculty of the soul, is not contemplated. . . . Any conception of autonomy is quite foreign to Plato's understanding of man.[3]

---

2. See Cornford, *Plato's Cosmology*, 'What Comes About of Necessity', 47e–48e.
3. See R. E. Cushman, *Therapeia*, chap. III, 4.

This is based on a narrow view of the question, which derives from the fact that Plato did not have the terminology that was later created by Christian doctrine for this subject, and that he simply took this possibility for granted. The best answer to this objection is simply the manifest motivation behind Plato's work as a whole, which was aimed at persuading men to stop living beneath themselves morally and intellectually, by dispelling their false beliefs. No one who disbelieved in what we call free will could have done such a thing. If we tell our readers that "the unexamined life" is not worth living, we must take for granted that they are free to begin examining it, if our statement is to have any purpose. (There can be no real choices without self-determination.)

Further on in the same place, the same commentator admits an essential condition for free will, despite the above:

> By "voluntary"' he specifies an inherent and pristine affection of the *psuche*, its real *eros*. By "involuntary", he means the suppression and inhibition of this *eros* by an encroaching and contrary affection of lower rank.[4]

That mankind is constantly liable to be "governed and enslaved by an inferior preference,"[5] which can be overcome by knowledge, is a recurrent Platonic theme which should serve to confirm Plato's belief in free will.

The scope of free will as seen by Plato is more confined than are modern ideas of it, inasmuch as it is conceived to function between just two fundamental alternatives, or orders of reality. Nevertheless, even here, the wider possibilities of free will would seem to be implicit in the higher of these two directions of choice. Plato calls for the "conversion" of the soul as insistently as Christianity, as in *Republic*, book VII, 525, "an easier conversion of the soul itself from becoming to truth and being." Cushman says that the words for "conversion" (*epistrophe*) or "to convert" occur at least twenty-one times in Book VII alone of the *Republic*.[6] This says enough for the

4. Cushman, ibid.
5. Cushman, ibid.
6. *Therapeia*, chap. VI, 3.

implicit commitment to free will, and it now remains to be seen what it was based on.

The theory of forms has the ethical consequence of confronting man with two orders of reality in personal experience, both competing for his allegiance. To explain why the desires should be converted from the material to the intelligible among these realities, is the primary aim of the *Timaeus*, in relation to man's origins. This dialogue develops to the full an idea which is implicit in the theory of forms, that reason is a primal reality, and that the material world is subsequent to it. This is an exact inversion of the order in which the world is customarily viewed by common sense, according to which the intelligence arrives both historically and biographically after prolonged developments on other levels.

Because of these natural appearances, it is often thought that the cultivation of reason is just a matter of taste among a minority, in a way which does not distinguish it from sports and hobbies, and not a matter of concern for the meaning of everyone's existence. To confound such attitudes, Plato wrote a cosmology based on that of the Pythagorean, Timaeus of Locri, from whom it received its name, in which reason is active from the beginning in the person of the Demiurge, who is shown creating everything most akin to intelligence, prior to the material world. The main divisions of the dialogue are the Works of Reason, the Works of Necessity, and the Co-operation of Reason and Necessity. It shows Plato to be as much a follower of Pythagoras as of Socrates.

Although freedom is not referred to there as such, Plato's continual opposition of reason to necessity (*ananke*) leaves little room for doubt that it is in reason that the essence of freedom is envisaged. This conception shows that no conflict is felt between freedom and obedience to law, albeit law of a metaphysical order. Mere caprice or chance are, strangely to us, assimilated to necessity. The conjunction of these things is also important here because if the physical world, the world of necessity, is also the world of chance, the pattern of causality must be discontinuous of itself, making it open to the intervention in it of man's will.

The Two Rival Powers

The origin of the realm of necessity and chance is said to reside in the substratum from which, or in which, the world was made. This is the original chaos or "nurse of becoming",[7] which is to be wrought into order and form by the action of the ideal-forms. As the "receptacle of becoming", it is the third reality in order after the intelligible and eternal model, and its visible and mutable copy. It is said to contain the four elements constantly changing into one another without rhyme or reason. Everything in it is in a state of constant chaotic vibratory and rectilinear motion. Such is the root of the inferiority of instantiated reality; a fixed receptacle would manifest the forms as they truly are, whereas their instances are deformed and corruptible owing to the instability of the material principle.

As this receptacle is devoid of intrinsic qualities, it can receive all of them and allow incoming ones to displace those already manifest in it. It is essentially intermediate between being and becoming, which makes it opaque to all logical thought, which operates wholly in relation to what is and what is not. From this proceeds much of what is meaningless in the visible world. Thus the eidetic realities are never able to secure any permanent foothold in it, or fully to master it, whence their instances always oppose, corrupt, and displace one another. This is why matter can only be reached by a kind of "bastard reason" (*logismo tini notho*), and why the intelligible falls between the material world and the One or the Good. The indefiniteness of material things is significant, as their falling-short (*endeia*) of their forms is what shows that they are not ultimately real. Thus they are adequate to opinion, but not to intelligence. Were there no difference between opinion and intelligence, sensibles could be entirely real.[8]

According to J. N. Findlay, the necessity and chance in the world result from the forms' having eidetically appropriate relations to one another in their own realm, while this order is dissolved once

---

7. *Timaeus*, 52d.
8. Ibid., 51b–e.

they are instanced. Their instances can then form all kinds of combinations, including those with and without any eidetic meaning. The choice then is between a causality in the one case which is "integrated, eidetically based", and "eidetically irrelevant and instantially compresent," in the other.[9] Freedom would be where like related to like.

Such is the idea of the material which limits the power of the Demiurge by its intractability, and which has been taken by Cornford to mean that Plato's Demiurge was not really omnipotent. Previously, A. E. Taylor and Archer-Hind had argued that the Demiurge was God, and therefore omnipotent, and that the chaos resisting his action could therefore only be "a mere residuum of hitherto unexplained fact, which complete knowledge . . . would reduce to nothing."[10]

Cornford points out that nothing as insignificant as that could be the counterpart of reason, and that the limitation caused by the material principle must be real, but his conclusion that the Demiurge cannot be omnipotent is not necessary, as it ignores the possibility that omnipotence must allow all degrees of perfection and imperfection. Both Taylor and Cornford adhere unwittingly to an over-simple idea of omnipotence which would make it display itself in extraordinary feats all the time. But the complete expression of creative power requires the limited as much as the unlimited, and the greatest things cannot be improved by repetition.

The essential action of the Demiurge is to impart circular motion to this realm of chaotic motion, as this kind of motion is said to be the kind most expressive of intelligence. It is a perfect blending of motion with fixity, showing how the negative aspects of motion, i.e., dispersion, corruption, instability, can be removed from it, while it remains still obviously motion. Too much familiarity should not blind us to its extraordinary quality in reconciling motion and rest, together with an infinite range of speeds in one motion. This resolves the elements into inorganic bodies, which is followed by the creation of living organisms, and that in turn by human beings, in whom the whole process becomes conscious.

9. *Plato: The Written & Unwritten Doctrines*, chap. VIII, iv. (p. 319).
10. F. M. Cornford, *Plato's Cosmology*, Reason & Necessity, 47e-48e, pp. 164–165.

Thus the universe is a mixed result of reason and necessity, and the vital statement is as follows: "Reason overruled Necessity by persuading her to guide the majority of those things which become towards what is best; in that way and on that principle this universe was constructed in the beginning by the victory of rational persuasion over Necessity."[11] It will be seen that man's acquisition of rationality is modelled on the formation of the world itself. The order of nature and the rationality of the perceiver have a common origin.

Modes of Necessity

Superficially, what is contained in the above is contradictory. Necessity means for us that which must be, come what may, and to speak of its being overruled would seem merely to transfer the property of necessity from it to whatever overruled it. The answer lies in the ancient conception of necessity in union with chance as mentioned earlier. While it admits the internal necessity in causal processes, it also allows the idea that each such process or series may be one great contingency. This conception can be applied to today's world as well, because it is obvious that if a machine is switched on, a continuous causal series will be manifest in its action by necessity, whereas this necessity in no way extends to our switching it on in the first place.

There is therefore nothing contradictory in the idea of a realm of discontinuous necessity, with its openness to a contingent variety of agencies. Its essential reality is not so much that of laws as that of the ideal-forms, the intelligible action of which cannot be bound by relations between their instances. Causality as a short-range phenomenon is explicitly present in the *Timaeus*: "If I wish to recover a debt, I may have to sail to Aegina to find my debtor; but nothing compels me to sail. The necessity lies in the links connecting the purposing will at the beginning of the chain with the attainment of the purpose at the end; *we need not think of it extending further in either direction*."[12]

11. *Timaeus*, 48a.
12. *Plato's Cosmology*, Reason & Necessity, 47e–48e, pp. 174–175 (my emphasis).

Plato and the Possibility of Free Will

The world may thus be full of potential causal agents, only a fraction of which are brought into action at any time. The termini of causal chains could be called causal voids, or areas of contingency.

Natural causes in this context are conceived as "errant causes", that is, they are all such as produce their effects in a purely robotic manner; regardless of conditions or suitability. Thus a fire may warm a room or burn the house down, without any change in its nature, and likewise a carpenter's tools may carve his timber or cut his throat. The errant causes obey laws, but the sum total of their activities is lawless unless some other principle governs the occasions on which they act, this being reason, mediated by the soul. Consequently, the ideas of chance, necessity, and nature are always closely related, because the vital ingredient of intelligent purpose is absent from such things by their very nature. As such, they cannot explain anything.

This incompleteness of nature is a result of the chaos on which it is founded, an idea where Plato differs deeply from Kant, for whom the external world is wholly the manifestation of the noumenon, and for whom all causal action was continuous. Another vital difference here is that, on Plato's principles, the entry of rational causality into natural causal processes is not something desirable simply from a human point of view; rather it is necessary if there is to be an ordered world at all, as will be shown later. Nevertheless, there is a general similarity between Platonic and Kantian views on this subject, as the efficient causality of natural phenomena is the delegated causality of the forms for Plato, and the manifestation of the noumenon, for Kant. In neither case does the higher causal principle have to act on something alien when it produces changes among things instanced from it in the external world. Rather, it is more a case of the causal principle modifying its own previous productions.

In both cases also, the intelligence is the causal principle which acts on the natural plane, but the Platonic view includes both its action upon this world, and its action in the mythical creation by the Demiurge. In the latter, reason acts on the primal chaos and imposes order on the random motion. This is logically, and possibly temporally, the first of the two exercises of rational causal power, although it is possible for them to be simultaneous. Any secondary ordering action upon nature by reason will therefore be manifest as an increase of order, as reason necessarily works in a way that reflects the eidetic order of which it is part.

One thing common to both these levels of causality is that the "persuasion" of Necessity by Reason means the redirection and qualification of blind motion and force, though *their* necessity is not to be equated with that of laws of science. In this context, all such laws are instances of ideal-forms, and therefore by definition wholly posterior to the original "persuasion" of Necessity. Nevertheless, the things which act under these laws display the "errant" character already discussed.

The original necessity of chaos is a thing of pure disorder, but it is unable to resist the influence of reason and the forms, because any such resistance could only be possible by means of a stability and uniformity such as only the presence of the forms could give, and which are by definition absent. While its lack of form makes it unable to exclude reason, however, it cannot entirely accept it either, because if it were wholly assimilable to form, it would effectively be a form.

Plato is not a monist, and the idea of the alien nature of the instantial world is central to his thought. This can be seen if the forms are compared with the soul: as the forms are to the primal matter, so is rational soul to the world which results from the union of forms with matter. Here we have the basis for the significance attributed to the choice of priorities between material and intelligible realms, and its consequences for freedom. Two "ontological directions" are defined by the gulf between forms and their instances, according as the free agent either follows intelligible reality in the direction of its source, or in the direction of its self-diffusion in the material, away from unity to multiplicity. This is a way of understanding the realms of Reason and Necessity.

These relationships are prefigured in the hierarchical order among the forms themselves, and their manifestation in the material world tends at its lower culmination to a sheer nullity which is in no way attainable by the forms, but only by their material instances. Man's power of choice in this connection depends on his having a rational soul. If this soul were simply something peculiar to human beings, however, it might not suffice for the role assigned it, so the conception of it is universalized by means of the account of the creation outlined above, in relation to the Works of Reason.

A Human and Cosmic Order

Not only is soul not exclusively human, but it is said to be the first thing created, the Soul of the World, which is the pattern of the world and the archetypal living being. The rational human soul is qualitatively of the same nature as it, and this is said to be joined to its body by the mediation of the irrational soul, which is said to be created by the lesser divinities, along with the body. This account of man's creation is most important as it involves the idea of man as a microcosmos, as his formation can be seen to be a recapitulation on a vastly reduced scale of the creation of the world.

The same point is also emphasized by the attribution to man of individual circulations corresponding to those of the Same and the Different in the universe. At birth, man's share of the Different makes havoc with his share of the Same, the rational principle, but the latter is always free to reassert itself in time. Analogies are drawn between the alternations of the cosmic circulations described in the *Statesman* dialogue, and those in the life of man. The title of this section in the *Timaeus* is the Co-Operation of Reason and Necessity, which would not only be a metaphysical definition of man, but would show that Plato considered these two realities not to be mutually destructive, but capable of constructive interaction.

As the world was created by the imposition of Reason on Necessity, so man, as microcosm, completes the process of his own creation by reproducing this ascendancy of reason in his own development. The gradual enlargement of his rationality is in a certain sense a reascent along the way whence the constituents of his being have come. Such would be the positive sense of the "ontological direction" referred to above. Since reason is declared to be the primary cause of the world, it is clear that increase of rationality must also mean an increase in causal power, the latter being an essential concomitant of freedom. Reason belongs to the realm of formal causality, which is logically and ontologically prior to that of efficient causality, which consists only in such powers as mechanical force, solidity, heating and cooling. The intelligible reaches the most essential form of causality.

This choice of possibilities for the human soul would not exist if it occupied either a higher or a lower position in the scheme of things. Its freedom of choice comes of its being a mediator. It is a typical Platonic principle that disparate realities are united by means, and soul mediates between indivisible and eternal realities and those which are completely divisible and subject to constant change in corporeal form. As the third between these two, it is called a "self-moving number". Self-motion means it is unmoved from without, like the forms, while its self-motion connects it with the moving and alter-motive world. Likewise it relates to the former by being non-spatial, and to the latter by being temporal. The union of opposites like fixity and motion by circular motion is a very apt symbol of its function, therefore.

Its self-motion goes beyond mere local motion, as it has also a movement from ignorance to knowledge by recollection (*anamnesis*) of the forms. There is an analogy between this and mathematical reality, because that too mediates between the intelligible and the sensible, and so has quasi-instantiation. But mathematical principles mediate only under the aspect of the One and the Many; soul also does this, but also under that of Motion and Rest. There is an unresolved problem here, in that soul is taken to be subordinate to the forms, although it is a center of independent action and consciousness, whereas the forms seem to be simply transcendental objects. To excel soul in every respect, forms would have to have their own eidetic equivalent of change and activity, as is suggested by Plato elsewhere.[13] Reason is established primarily in the World Soul, and from thence into the natural order. As reason is in soul, so soul is "in" body, by which means man can identify with the reality next in order above his own place in nature, and share in its causality and freedom, if he will.

On the one hand, the power of passion and sensation is present in man simply from his being present in the world, but on the other, this

13. *Sophist*, 249 b, c, d.

power can be matched by that of an *eros* directed to what can be recognized as something more essential in his being. In any case, every union of disparate principles implies the eventual dominance of one over the other. His soul is of like nature with the World Soul, and his body with the material world, whence he may imitate the universe, with his rational soul prevailing over necessity, or allow the unordered movements of sense and emotion to rule instead. The former course of action instances a universal *eidos*, whereas the latter seems either to have no such archetype, or a very insignificant one. If reason did not prevail on the cosmic scale, there would be no world in which man could learn to imitate the same order.

This idea of contrary forces in our nature, one of which is bound to dominate the other, is affirmed at various places in the *Timaeus*, as for example in the case where the soul may be dominated by the body:

> [W]hen a large body, too big for the soul, is conjoined with a small and feeble mind, whereas man's natural appetites are twofold—desire of food for the body and desire of wisdom for our divinest part—the motions of the stronger part prevail and, by augmenting their own power at the same time as they render that of the soul dull, slow to learn, and forgetful, they produce in her that worst of ailments, stupidity.[14]

The mere fact that Plato thinks it is an open question which side of this duality shall rule the other is a strong indication of an implicit belief in free will. The interplay of reason and physical necessity in the universe is thus manifest in the individual person. As if in confirmation that it is not a matter of chance which power prevails over the other, Plato connects this question with that of the soul's power of self-motion a little further on:

> [A]s regards motions, the best is *that produced by oneself in oneself* [my italics], since it is most nearly akin to the movement of thought in the universe. Motion effected by another is inferior;

---

14. Ibid., 88b, p. 129.

worst of all is that whereby external agents move separate parts of the body while the latter is completely at rest.[15]

To speak of such an independent power of self-motion scarcely differs from speaking of free will in so many words. Because human beings are composed from all the properties of the universe, they are capable of being moved in various ways from without, like inanimate objects, while their power of self-motion comes from the most spiritual part of their being, and that is what can rule the lower forms of motion.

Any doubt that rulership is intended, and that a rulership which concretely incorporates what thought can recognize as reason is dispelled in the next passage, where the terms "destined to govern" and "sovereignty" are used:

So much for the care of the living creature as a whole and of its bodily part, and for the way in which a man may best lead a rational life, both governing and being governed by himself. Still more should precedence be given to the training of *the part destined to govern* [my italics], in order that it may be as fully equipped as possible for its task of sovereignty.[16]

Without the element of self-transformation present in all this, the choice between the intelligible and the sensible realms could not have the importance Plato claims for it. One could as well seek the true good only in the changing sensory world as in the other, because its positive content is that of the forms in any case, albeit at second-hand, and they remain intelligible at that level. Thus the world of sense can be taken for the source of a knowledge comparable to a that of the intelligibles as such, but the implications for the individual differ profoundly.

The ordering process effected by the rational soul is also said to be reversed in the physical world with the passage of time in the *Statesman* dialogue, where it completes the picture given in the *Timaeus*, with its conception of God repeatedly re-creating the

15. Ibid., 89a, p.130.
16. Ibid., 89d, p.131.

world and then leaving it to its own devices, upon which it steadily runs down in increasing disorder until it has to be recovered from the edge of chaos by another re-creation. The world's circulations are turned in opposite directions at each of these junctures, just as man's own equivalent of these circulations are reversed at his being born, while being able to revert to their former directions with the passage of time.

The periodic reversals on earth are experienced as great upheavals, both in the world and in the individual, and it may be noted that the decline into disorder is also to be taken together with what was said about the tendency of the instances of the forms to move and combine in patterns that have no eidetic basis. The history of a created world is therefore paralleled by that of mankind, but there is an important difference as well:

> The subsequent history of the Universe is parallel to that of man, but there is a difference. The Universe goes from good to bad, and from bad to worse: so therefore does the race of man. . . . Be our archons never so perfect, the ageing world will make their state decay. But, as for the individual, it rests with him, or rather with his educators, what his fate shall be: let him aspire 'to correct the cerebral cycles corrupted at birth, by studying the harmonies and cycles of the Universe, and to assimilate the knowing part to the known as it originally was.'[17]

Reason the Key to Freedom

This brings out Plato's identification of reason with freedom, because any given individual can escape the predetermined cosmic process, and so may have freedom, insofar as this freedom is achieved in the development of reason, the correction of the cerebral cycles. Such a perspective could be acceptable from a scientific point of view as well, because science has shown by the Second Law of Thermodynamics that every process in nature is impelled by the

---

17. James Adam, *The Nuptial Number of Plato*, part 2, sec. 6, p. 81.

breakdown of ordered matter and the dissipation of available energy, irreversibly. While science has nothing to say about the ascending, creative, part of the myth, we may presume its existence, as it would be hard to see how there still could be a world at all if there were nothing to punctuate the universal run-down. By means of these ideas, the pursuit of reason is released from being just a personal preoccupation, and becomes a vital means whereby man makes known his spiritual soul which transcends his individuality, in a way which effects a stabilizing union between mankind and its Origin which strengthens the order of the world.

Plato's most direct reference to free will and its consequences for the individual is to be found in the final myth of Book X of the *Republic*. It is the vision of the afterlife seen by Er the Armenian, who is said to have been killed in battle and to have been restored to life to recount his experiences of the afterlife. The disembodied souls are said to have a vision of the whole macrocosm, with its multiple motion about a luminous axis, which is attached to the spindle of Necessity. Necessity and the Fates appear to rule everything. The souls in the afterlife are told that a new cycle of existence lies before them, and that each must make its choice from among all the possible lives, each with its attendant angel. Every choice once made is said to bind the chooser to it by necessity, but this is balanced by the assertion that "virtue has no master," (*Rep.* X, 617E) and that how much of this virtue one has depends only on how much one esteems it. The responsibility for the choices is said to rest entirely on the souls, not on God or the Fates, showing an implicit conviction as to their free will. The use of their freedom is binding on them, however, as "the soul becomes different according as it chooses a different life," and many are said to choose without examining the life closely enough, often simply as an unreflecting reaction to past experiences.

When the choice of life is made irrevocably, the souls are led to the plain of Lethe, where they drink from the river of Forgetfulness. Then at midnight they are sent to their births in the material world. If this myth is interpreted in the manner indicated by Plotinus, it can be used to account both for the soul's freedom with regard to the different kinds of life it could have in this world, and for explaining the interaction between freedom and necessity. Plotinus does not take literally the transmigratory aspect of the text, as shown by the following:

> But if the presiding Spirit and the conditions of life are chosen by the Soul in the over-world, how can anything be left to our independent action here? The answer is that that very choice in the over-world is in fact an allegorical statement of the Soul's tendency and temperament, a total character which it must express wherever it operates.... The Soul's quality exists before any bodily life.... Where we read that, after the casting of the lots the choice is made upon vision, in accordance with the individual temperament, we are given to understand that the real determination lies with the souls, who adapt the allotted conditions to their own particular quality.[18]

The myth can thus be taken as a vivid illustration of the intrinsic freedom of the personality, which can commence its interactions with the world as freely as if it had no embodiment at all. (The literal sense of Plato's myth would in any case be as useless as the advice to choose one's parents carefully.) The concept of freedom connecting itself with fate, as presented here, can be linked to what was said above about the idea of natural causality as a short-range phenomenon. One's recovery of a debt entails a series of necessary actions, but the commencement of it is not necessary. Causal sequences binding on individuals are always more or less limited; now either man is wholly a part of the natural order or he is not. If he is, the finite lengths of human causal sequences are a sample of a causal process throughout nature; if he is not wholly a part of the natural order, there would be no reason for him to be bound by universal causality in any case.

The same principle applies, whether a whole life were chosen from outside the physical world as such, or simply a different course of action within it, since the mysterious devolution of freedom into determination is the same in either case. This devolution is an effect of the great excess of causal potential over outlets for effects which

18. *Enn.* III, 4, 5.

will be discussed later. The causality of choice therefore transfers one necessarily to a more restricted realm.

However, in *Republic* X, Plato is not verbally consistent, inasmuch as he there uses the word Necessity in a sense much more like that which it has for modern science than the one it had in his description of Chaos in the *Timaeus,* where it was subject to persuasion. In the latter case, it was a reality prior to all instantiated realities, while in the scientific sense it is a property of the world which, according to Plato, has resulted from the instancing of the forms, and is integral to the cosmic order.

Necessity in the more scientific sense of the word follows logically from the nature of a world which functions in a completely uniform manner, on the macrocosmic scale, at least, as Plato thought it did. Necessity is inseparable from uniformity. Such is the necessity which is said to be symbolized by the cosmic spindle, and to be manifest in all the different lots or possible lives, which could as well be called different causal series, running more or less parallel. It is essential to this passage that free will and necessity are equally real and capable of coexistence, with many degrees of interaction. The externally verifiable determination by the lot chosen before birth is balanced by what Plato calls virtue, which "has no master." The latter involves an inner freedom from the contents of sense, because of which the real good is not found in, but only through, the sensory world. This is a potentiality which is to be realized by the moral virtues.

Therefore the freedom implied by the Platonic virtue does not of itself remove any of the necessary causes acting on the chosen life, but it does mean that the relation of these things to the individual can be transformed from within, in proportion as the center of the will's action is directed to the intelligible formal causes behind the efficient causes that rule in the visible world, so participating in the former. In practice, that is not as abstruse as it sounds, because the choice involved is experienced by most people in the possibility of commitment to values, even if not to God as well. Here is where this metaphysical conception of the will's action finds its universality. The universal values have an immediate relevance for innumerable persons who have never thought of them in connection with Platonism or any theoretical system.

According to the Myth of Er, however, the two directions of the soul's activity are not equally determined. On the one hand, it is compelled to choose some part or other of the material world, conformably with the necessity which prevails there, but on the other hand, it is under no compulsion to exert itself in the direction of freedom, because freedom must be freely chosen. The will's entry into the material world of causation resembles the instantial movement of the forms, inasmuch as it thus binds itself to a state of interaction, without for all that being contained like a passenger in a vehicle. Its entry into this state transforms a part of its freedom into unfreedom.

This means that the individual has the choice of being as nearly as possible wholly determined by the external, or of transforming the action of the things which determine him, by means of a certain transformation of himself, thus changing the kind of being upon which they act. Here freedom appears under more than one aspect. The one that counts in this connection is the "static" potentiality of free will, which acts in its own dimension regardless of the uses made of its dynamic potentiality in regard to practical options. This is the division referred to in the text, where man is at once "bound by necessity", while also having that which "has no master".

The Two Ways

The form of freedom I have called static is as it were the "independent variable" in relation to the other. Power of choice in given situations depends on a subsistent freedom which transcends all particular applications, but for Plato in *Republic* X, the will's power to initiate new causal series seems to be limited to its power to transfer itself from one pre-existing causal series or "lot" to another. Free will *enters*, but does not *originate*, new causal series in the myth, rather after the manner of a change of career, as where a soldier, say, might change to being an engineer.

The will's power over different causal series seems *prima facie* to be limited to this, which would be simply a power to become subject to different causal series, but not to originate them. The question, then, is whether this text may also imply that the will can also

31

initiate causal series? I think this is implicit in what it says. If the will has the causal agency to transfer itself from one causal series to another, this agency must extend to at least some things other than its own internal states, for if it did not, the implication would be that the will's choice was not real at all, in which case the "new" series would be just a continuation of the old one, contrary to the hypothesis of this text.

Granted this degree of effectuality among externals, then, we have no reason to deny that the will can also cause new beginnings. The operation of the will for Plato can therefore be analyzed into three domains: (1) The wholly inward, where mind and will are focused on intelligibles. (2) The passively outward, where it accedes to options from among those imposed on it. (3) The actively outward, where the will initiates new sequences from itself.

In his commentary on this text, Proclus endorses the voluntaristic interpretation, and elaborates it by taking the plain of Lethe and its waters as an allegory of the material world. To the latter, he opposes the Plain of Truth in the *Phaedrus* as an antitype,[19] one which is said to correspond to the highest part of the soul, where it has direct vision of the forms. His account of the descent of the souls at "midnight" is taken as an assimilation between materiality and the oblivion of darkness. The implication is that the loss of truth is never altogether involuntary, any more than its acquisition. Proclus also adds an argument for free will at this point, based on the fact that there are persons who rightly or wrongly assert the reality of free will. There are then two possibilities, (a) that they behave like this of themselves, in which case they have free will, or (b) that they are compelled to do so by a causal principle which determines everything. In the latter case this principle is in conflict with itself, and hence it must leave room for freedom.

However, the main theoretical weight of Plato's implicit doctrine on free will remains in the *Timaeus,* where, as in the *Philebus* argument, man's material part is taken from the matter of the universe, while his moral and intellectual principles are derived from those parts of the universe which correspond to them. (The harmonic

19. *In Rep.* X, XVI, 259–261, Festugiere, tr.

divisions of the Soul imply that the arts attain to the nature of things with as much right as the sciences). The *Timaeus* conception of man and the soul is still relevant for science. What happens in the remotest star is still happening in a way which corresponds to man's reason, and the same applies at the opposite extreme in the sub-atomic realm.

Our ability to understand such remote things can directly be accounted for by reason's being built into the structure of the universe before some of it was acquired by mankind. Such a point of view has appeared in modern philosophy of science:

> Nevertheless, by insisting that the Universe is rational — which really means that the Universe has a causal structure which can be ordered by the human mind, and further that the ultimate reason for the existence of the Universe can be understood by human beings — the defenders of the cosmological argument are taking an Anthropic Principle position. In its insistence that there is an actual hierarchy of causes in the Universe which is isomorphic with the pyramid of causes constructed by human beings, the cosmological argument is analogous to the teleological argument, for the latter argument asserts that the order observed in the Universe is isomorphic to the order produced by human beings when they construct artifacts. In both arguments, the mental activities of human beings are used as a model for the Universe as a whole.[20]

This degree of correspondence looks less and less accidental, in which case, the scientific objection to finding anything to do with purpose, moral value, or beauty in the Universe, may not in itself be very scientific.

Plato's conception of man in the *Timaeus* allows only a limited idea of free will. Man is seen as poised between rival forces which aim at mastery over his will. The life ruled by reason, and the life ruled by hedonism and materialism are the extremes between which it can vary, but not much room is allowed for anything more spontaneous or creative, such as the writing of Plato's philosophy

20. Barrow and Tipler, *The Anthropic Cosmological Principle*, chap. 2, 9.

itself. He may have made the will's scope look more limited than he really believed it to be, so as to emphasize what was most essential for it. This involves the Socratic-Platonic idea of the moral will as a condition of metaphysical knowledge. Disbelief in metaphysical realities will be a foregone conclusion (see Cushman, above), if the whole bent of the will is towards the material and the transient. Hence the need for a moral *therapeia* to adjust mind and will to their most important objects.

Other implications follow from this idea of the relation of the moral and the intellectual. The materially-dominated direction of the will can rightly be called evil for the further reason that it is a very false friend to the natural life when it becomes the exclusive concern of that life. This is because everything in the material realm is either in the process of coming into existence by aggregation or passing out of it again by disintegration. There is no third state besides these two, whence every existent in this realm is, in relation to it, a collection of raw material from which yet others are to be made. The more free the material order is to act according to its own property, therefore, the more complete is the rule of mutability and corruptibility, therefore.

Thus the direction of the will and its desires towards the sensory world is an assimilation of the person to forces of change, irresistible on that level, for which he is simply material for yet more beings. This is ethically neutral as a cosmic law, but humanly speaking, it can only be regarded as destructive evil, irreconcilable with anything recognizable as freedom, whether for individuals or whole societies.

In summary, the Platonic conception of free will depends on two things, namely, the metaphysics of the forms, with the profound ontological difference between them and the world of sensibles, and secondly, the formation of man as a microcosm. Being an epitome of both of these orders of realities, man is, so to speak, constructed around this ultimate duality, without his being intrinsically identified with either. The actualization of freedom comes through a self-identification with the intelligible side of the *eidos*-instance combination.

2

Plotinus and the
Essence of Freedom

The Neoplatonic Background

This philosophical successor to Plato, whose name is curiously similar to Platonos, lived some six hundred years after Plato, and this separation in time calls for some remarks on Plotinus' background, and on the tradition he represents. His concern with free will is almost wholly intellectual and mystical, not political or social, partly because in his lifetime, 204–270 AD, political activity was monopolized by the Roman imperial power. Not much is known about him personally, because he discouraged questions about himself and his origins, but Proclus referred to him as "Plotinus the Egyptian",[1] and it is also asserted by Eunapius that he came from Lycopolis (Assiut) in Egypt.

However, he was a Greek at least culturally, and possibly racially, and studied philosophy first at Alexandria, where he was taught by Ammonius Saccas for eleven years. Ammonius did not write anything, but his ideas are known through those of another student called Origen (not the Church Father), whose writings survive. Nevertheless, it is believed that the Christian Origen was also a student of Ammonius, besides having been taught by Clement of Alexandria.

Plotinus had family connections with senatorial families in Rome, thanks to whose influence he obtained permission to accompany Gordian III's expedition against Persia, so that he could study Eastern doctrines. After Gordian was murdered during the campaign,

---

1. Plat. Theol., I, 1.

Plotinus managed to make his way to Rome, where his social connections secured him the use of a house from a wealthy widow, Gemina, where he studied and taught, and where his students included members of the Senate.[2]

It is with Plotinus that Neoplatonism is said to begin, because so little is known of his immediate predecessors, while his own writings and those of his successors survive plentifully. However the prefix "Neo-" is misleading because it gives the impression that Platonism had died out, only to be revived in the 3rd and 4th centuries AD. But the mere lack of original Platonic writings surviving from between Plato's time and that of Plotinus, cannot be taken as proof of this. On the contrary, the writings of Philo of Alexandria (20 BC–AD 50) are proof that Platonism was a sufficiently vital intellectual force in that part of the world in the 1st century AD to profoundly influence an orthodox Jewish philosopher:

> He was a convinced and ardent Platonist. . . . At the same time he cherished a deep and devoted loyalty to his ancestral tradition, and believed he could bridge the chasm that seemed to sunder the Greek and Jewish realms from one another.[3]

This evidence for the influence of Platonism two hundred years before Plotinus should therefore cast doubt on the view of his philosophy as being simply a revival. Nevertheless, the term Neoplatonism legitimately denotes a new increase in the importance of this kind of philosophy, and its diffusion to a wider audience, partly because of the genius of Plotinus himself, and partly because of a universal change in the early centuries AD among the leaders of thought, and among all those who were sensitive to the change of mental climate, towards a more speculative and otherworldly point of view. St. Augustine's *City of God,* and Proclus' *Commentary on Plato's Republic,* where what is written of the mystical Book X is equal to his work on the first nine books together, are eloquent witnesses to this change.

The supplanting of small kingdoms and city states by the Roman

---

2. J. M. Rist, *Plotinus–The Road to Reality,* chap. 2.
3. *Philo of Alexandria,* David Winston, tr., introduction, p. 1.

Plotinus and the Essence of Freedom

Empire, and the freedom of movement within it left large and growing numbers of people without the support of their traditional communities and customs. This made many of them more willing to look inward for a spiritual security for which the outside world could give no equivalent, whence they became receptive to metaphysics or Christianity, or both. This development is usually taken to be all part of the decline of the Roman Empire, because of the great numbers of those who did not react to it constructively, but simply took it for a removal of moral restraints.

But although the decline was real, on the broadest scale, it was not an undiluted evil. There is always some state, desirable in itself, which must decline or cease in order that another, related to a more authentic consciousness, may arise. Every breakdown of a culture is also an opening through which a way back to its spiritual foundations can be found by those who are alert for it. The metaphysical awakening of this period would thus be the one thing which ran counter to the general decline, and while not being widespread enough to reverse or halt it, it subtly changed its meaning and created an intellectual heritage for future centuries which ensured the continuity of Platonic thought.

Plotinus was both philosopher and mystic, and, according to Porphyry's biography, he attained a vision of the One on at least four occasions during his life. Besides this, philosophy for him was inseparable from the kind of self-identification with the intellect which we have already considered as one of the fundamental directions open to man's free will according to the *Timaeus*. The dialectical operations of philosophy were expected to disclose the real nature of the thinker himself, which included a theoretical knowledge of the immortality of the soul. Plotinus' practice was to concentrate the mind on knowledge of this kind until it became more than just theoretical, and became the subject of a direct experience. For this reason, Plotinus' mystical-philosophical tendency could be called "gnostic" in the broadest sense of the word, despite the fact that he was deeply opposed to the sects under that name which arose in those times, and wrote a long tractate against them.[4]

4. *Enn.* II, 9.

Gnosticism denied the elements of truth and goodness in the world, which philosophical argument depends on.

Doubts About Free Will

In one passage where Plotinus introduces free will,[5] he indicates an important psychological reason for the widespread and perennial doubts entertained about the freedom of the will. It arises from the lively emotional impact made on us by so many of the unchangeable realities of life which ignore our wills: our birth, our growth into the forms we now have, the limits of our faculties, the dependence of our wills on many externals, our common mortality, and confinement within narrow limits of time and space. Such things can create a feeling that what depends on one's will is dwarfed into insignificance, if it exists at all. This ensures that fatalism will be an ever-recurrent attitude, always requiring the intervention of reason to evince the equal reality of freedom which coexists with it.

Elsewhere, however,[6] the argument for free will is based on the same facts that are instanced by determinists, the cases where we know our wills are forced by alien pressures, and where such pressures may take over completely. For this purpose, he makes a bold use of paradox, which exposes the idea of total determination, which he admits for the sake of argument, only to show its results are contradictory:

> But such an extremity of determination, a destiny so all-pervasive, *does away with the destiny that is affirmed:* it shatters the sequence and co-operation of causes.[7]

Not only does the experience of the will's being obliged to yield to something external not prove the nullity of the will, it rather proves that the will is a real agent. If it were not, there never would be any sense of resistance, in which case the determining agent would not deserve the name, since it would not be determining anything real.

5. *Enn.* VI, 8, 1.
6. *Enn.* III, 1, 4.
7. Ibid.

On the other hand, a universal determination with individual agents to act upon, could be real enough as determination, but it could not be absolute, because this would require that a measure of determination be allowed to the agents themselves.

Without this share of agency or causal power in individual subjects, then, the universal determination could not justify its name, as it would then be impossible to say what, if anything, it was doing. It might as well be powerless, because in this case, no power could ever be required of it. The reservation of all power to a single agent is therefore contradictory, as it would remove everything in regard to which it could have any function or purpose; active powers presuppose reactive ones. Causal sequences would be "shattered" in that nothing real was effected by them, as the Agent vanishes with the patients.

This conclusion invites comparison with an argument used by Hume from the opposite point of view,[8] to the effect that if the idea of freedom were taken so far as to nullify causality, it would be no more possible to hold anyone responsible for his actions than if there were no freedom at all; the free agent must still have causal power over his actions if his freedom is to be real. This is another example of how freedom and causality are complementary, and not contradictory.

If, in Plotinus' example, determinism was all, the result would be purely monistic:

> it is not a truth that all happens by causes, there is nothing but a rigid unity. We are no "we": nothing is our act ... we are no more agents than our feet are kickers when we use them to kick with.[9]

The fact that no one ever believes any such thing is taken for an argument in itself. Thus freedom must be able to cause things, while at the same time causality must be distributed in such a way that different beings can dispose of it independently, that is, have freedom. Once we are assured of the reality of the voluntary agent,

8. *Enquiry Concerning Human Understanding*, sec. VIII, part II.
9. *Enn.* III, 1, 4.

it is said that his act is characteristically produced "under no compulsion, and with knowledge."[10] These two conditions are associated by Plotinus, and they seem to be the only ones necessary, but Plotinus presses the requirement for knowledge to the extreme, with the result that for him, most actions which would be freely-willed for common sense could only be partially free.

This follows from the Platonic conception of knowledge, which confines it to the conceptual plane and denies it to sensibles. The example of Oedipus' killing of his father is alluded to in this connection, as a gross example of how the absence of knowledge annuls free will. Ignorance of the identity of the victim makes the killing an unfree act, but this point is followed by the question as to whether ignorance of the evil of murder itself was also something which could make the act unfree or involuntary. It could be said that the murderer had a duty to learn the truth about murder, but it could be said again that he was ignorant of the duty to learn.

This argument is not typical of Plotinus, whose main contention is for a knowledge of truths innate in us, as where he says: "Virtue is ours by the ancient staple of the Soul; vice is due to the commerce of the Soul with the outer world."[11] On this basis, he could have argued that actions could always be made involuntary by ignorance of matters of fact, such as the identity of a person, whereas ignorance of something universal, like the culpability of murder, could only occur through the suppression of something innate in us, and could therefore be as culpable in its way as the crime itself. We find the reality of culpability to be deduced directly from man's status as a real causal agent, which was proved by the argument from total determination outlined above.

A Source of Free Will

The Plotinian idea of free will is closely connected with the presence in us of something of an immaterial nature, "the unembodied". One of his crucial doctrines in this regard is that:

10. *Enn.* VI, 8, 1.
11. *Enn.* II, 3, 8.

Even our human Soul has not sunk entire; something of it is continuously in the Intellectual Realm, though if that part, which is in this sphere of sense, hold the mastery, or rather be mastered here and troubled, it keeps us blind to what the upper phase holds in contemplation.[12]

The Intellectual-Principle in us is held to be typical of our incorporeal part, and it would follow logically from our possession of such a reality that the forces and changes of the material world would not be able directly to affect it or determine it, as like can only act on like. The idea that man has a separable soul which differs fundamentally from the material of the body is essential to this idea of free will, therefore.

Modern trends in philosophy have made this kind of thinking look like an appeal to a *deus ex machina* or even a "ghost in the machine", but it should be remembered that the Platonic argument is based on an evaluation of the concreteness of the body which differs profoundly from that of common sense. The idea of concreteness or substantiality in use here is bound up wholly to its accessibility to knowledge. Ideas are capable of exact and permanent relations, and are therefore fully knowable, and therefore, in Platonic terms, fully concrete, as the truly real is *a priori* the conceptually clear. Material things, on the other hand, are constantly changing and incomplete, a flux of surfaces and fragmentary aspects about which one can have only opinion, and which are therefore insubstantial according to the same criterion as before.

Plotinus gives an original presentation of this common Platonic position[13] where he deduces the paradox that the matter "on which the universe rises" is a "non-existence". He defends it on the grounds that mountain and rock owe all their substantiality to their relations to things of like nature with themselves, and that their weight and downward force really imply a debility which cannot raise itself, which in turn is taken to imply unreality, as all the positive qualities are held to be inseparable. Debility may look strong

---

12. *Enn.* IV, 8, 8.
13. *Enn.* III, 6, 6–7.

against things of like nature. Material things scarcely impinge upon vital and intelligent ones, and this difference in concreteness is really to the credit of the latter, and not of the former as common sense takes it.

Where the separability of the soul is concerned, he argues directly against the Aristotelian idea of the soul[14] which would make it simply the entelechy of the body, the state of mutual adjustment of the body's parts and functions and proportions. This could lead to an infinite regress, it is inferred, because there would have to be yet another such being to set up this adjustment in the first place, rather as there must be a musician to tune the strings of an instrument.

Worse still, such a soul could not diverge in any way from the propensities of the body which, in reality, it "rules, guides, and often combats." Moreover, it could not be intelligent either, for although sense-perception could occur, there would be no basis for the independent inward function which is peculiar to intelligence; the motor-sensory input and output would account for everything in such a soul. Even sleep would be impossible, because the "withdrawal of the soul in sleep" would literally destroy the body if the two were as united as the form of a statue is with its metal or stone. Thus Plotinus is a consistent Platonist as regards both the separability as well as the relative concreteness of the soul. For him, the evaluations of the "ghost" and the "machine" would be reversed. Nevertheless, his reasoning supports the common sense idea of mind or soul controlling the body, despite being opposed to it in other respects.

This conception of the soul has consequences in regard to the kinds of activity in which freedom may be expressed. The separable soul which is superior to the body is itself subordinate to the Intellectual-Principle, which in turn is subordinate to the Good. From this it is concluded that activities in the material world, done for their own sake at least, cannot be regarded as truly free, however much they are so for common sense. Here, Plotinus introduces another criterion for freedom (in VI, 8), according to which the free act must be one which is motivated towards the intelligible good.

14. *Enn.* IV, 7, 8.

This means that it must have a final cause in something higher in the scale of values in respect of truth and moral and aesthetic value. It can be seen how this condition lowers the significance of all external options *per se,* which freedom is normally equated with.

This criterion counts as the third after man's being a real causal agent, and his possession of knowledge of all the circumstances of his action. They can be summarized therefore as: (1) (Causal agency; (2) Circumstantial knowledge; (3) Orientation to values. These conditions are obviously separable, but it is held that there is no full freedom of the will without all three. Mere causal agency could be operative, as with Oedipus killing his father, and in such cases there is neither circumstantial knowledge nor conscious intent toward values. The typical result of such actions is for the will to become the prisoner of other wills which act with a fuller range of the conditions. Such is the lowest expression of freedom.

The most typical case of free will embodies the first two conditions, where the individual is both a causal agent and a possessor of adequate knowledge relative to his action. This idea of free will is standard for practical affairs, and suffices for legal responsibility. But for Plotinus, even actions in this category are only half-free, because they belong necessarily in the material world, where they are involved in constant natural *accidentalia* and encounters with actions of like kind by other persons. Such activity in the outside world constantly confronts us with occasional causes for the operation of our wills, but without any proportionate scope for our initiative. Though the agency remains free in itself, it is thus also inevitably "a collaborator under compulsion," where the making of choices is inescapable.[15] All the active virtues are thus dependent on the play of circumstances, as bravery depends on disasters and dangerous conditions, justice requires injustices to be put right, the ability to teach requires encounters with ignorance, and generosity requires cases of need. The good doctor would prefer that nobody should need treatment.

The fullest degree of freedom is thus as little involved in action as is the least, though for different reasons. This symmetry between

15. *Enn.* vi, 8, 5.

43

these extremes comes from the fact that the unhindered potentiality for action can look like a state in which action is impossible anyway. But freedom means ultimately freedom in and for the Good.

What is deduced about the will is applied to the question as to how different people are allotted their different places in the world. It is even questioned whether the soul's presence in a body in this world might be the result of a choice of its own, despite the way in which a similar idea in *Republic* X was taken figuratively. Plotinus nevertheless believes in some kind of choice which takes place outside the series of choices we are conscious of making in regard to externals, and the language of reincarnation is sometimes used to illustrate his meaning.

A higher-level choice is thought to proceed from the qualitative nature of each being, because every quality is a form of determination which is coordinated in many ways with those of other beings, regardless of their simply conscious choices. For this reason, all beings find their places in the world through something like a magical attraction of like natures to like. That the physical relatedness of beings with a common quality should be a rule would seem to follow from the idea that every quality instances an ideal-form, which always remains a unity in itself. Thus the full instantiation of the form would imply not only the appearance of its quality in many beings, but also in a maximum of unity among those beings, so that the form's unity also may be instantiated as far as possible. Conversely, the more dispersed the instances are, the weaker is the instancing of each one of them.

Freedom's Causality

Moreover, qualities normally require some reflection in their surroundings if they are to develop, and that condition is met by the juxtaposition of like beings. In this way the instancing of forms would entail the coordination of the instances, with the result that changes in the qualities of any being will invisibly suppress one set of relations and create another one. Such is the metaphysics which provides a rationale for sympathetic magic, as in the artificial formation of relations with archetypal powers by a manipulation of symbols

44

bearing their qualities. Plotinus accepted this consequence, as he believed that magic was in essence something at work throughout nature, and this is why magic entered into the writings of a number of Renaissance Platonists, such as Ficino and Cornelius Agrippa.

Plotinus has no wish to commend magic, as for him it is the cause of the mind's deviations from the true good by fascinating its less rational powers: "Alone in immunity from magic is he who, though drawn by the alien parts of his total being, withholds his assent to their standards of worth...."[16] Its power of attraction is also the mechanism of retribution: "Anyone that adds his evil to the total of things is known for what he is and, in accordance with his kind is pressed down into the evil he has made his own, and hence, upon death, goes to whatever region fits his quality.... For the good man, the giving and the taking and the changes of state go quite the other way."[17]

This principle of attraction of like by like also appears in the use of reincarnationist explanations of life's mischances, such as the life of a slave resulting from a former life as an unjust ruler. Significantly, reincarnation is seldom used to explain *good* fortune, because that would have meant showing various forms of worldly prosperity as rewards for virtue, which would be unacceptable for the Plotinian idea of virtue. However, the idea of inescapable retribution conveyed by reincarnationist expressions is seriously meant, as it too is a consequence of the conception of *eide* and their instances.

All individual actions belong in the category of efficient causality, and they have therefore the power to change the part of the world where they occur. But no series of causes of this kind could continue for very long without the implication that the world could be permanently changed by efficient causality alone. The nature of every aspect of the world is, for Platonism, due to eternal, formal causes. In this case, every efficient causality may act either with or against the preestablished eidetic order, and if the tendency of the former is consistently opposed to the latter, the result will be a state of rising tension between the agent in question and the universal causality of

16. *Enn.* IV, 4, 44.
17. *Enn.* IV, 4, 45.

which he remains nevertheless a part. This can only be resolved by a series of actions with the contrary tendency. The destruction of the agent in question would not do this, it would only end the accumulation of disequilibria, while doing nothing to remove it. Therefore actions of a given quality can only be cancelled by actions of a contrary quality and tendency, and the eternity of the formal causes of the world makes this inescapable for all individuals; such is the kernel of truth conveyed by metaphors of reincarnation.

Self-destruction is always a possibility in this connection, because causal action which tends to annul the action of more universal causes must tend to this, because the agent is himself dependent on the causality he is trying to negate; this would apply equally to individuals and to nations. Such is the nature of evil, and it is clear that it cannot be freely-willed according to the full definition of freedom given above. It would be limited to causal agency and only a very partial knowledge of the circumstances, and nothing at all of the element of conscious orientation toward values. Evil actions are therefore never more than semi-free at their inception, and progress toward states where they are ever-increasingly under the power of alien causes, owing to which their freedom would tend almost to disappear.

The immortality of the soul is also relevant in this context, as it would be a means whereby one and the same individual could consciously rectify his own past actions in the light of the truth. This would be more meaningful than would be the case with reincarnation taken literally, where past actions are not known, with the result that no distinction can be made between the punishment of an offender and the punishment of an innocent bystander. But the necessity for this reckoning is not supposed to be binding on all men equally, whether with personal immortality or not. The conclusion drawn by R. T. Wallis is this regard is that "we can transcend the human level and identify ourselves with Intelligence, so escaping rebirth altogether,"[18] which certainly seems to be Plotinus' view of the matter in regard to those such as himself. There is never any indication that he has any expectation of being reborn in this world.

18. *Neoplatonism*, p. 72.

Plotinus and the Essence of Freedom

The question as to whether human lives are governed by astral influences is also discussed, and it is relevant to the present purpose because in Plotinus' time it was mainly in connection with astrology that the possibility of the will's being subject to natural forces was discussed. The tractate "Are the Stars Causes?" examines the popular belief that the stars are responsible for our worldly fortunes, and even virtues and vices as well. That stars could be benign because they are in one part of the sky and just the opposite because they are in another, is declared to be absurd.

On the other hand, he does not concede that they are lifeless and merely physical things either, because they are still acceptable as the locus of a generalized source of causal power. That seems to be as far as he will go, however, as he also remarks upon the fact that the planets are not really in the Zodiacal circle, but "considerably below it", showing that he was aware of the astronomers' objection that the planets are really nowhere near constellations in which they appear to move. Likewise, the idea of planetary aspects is also rejected on the grounds that beings cannot change their properties by changing their relations to one another.

This is below Plotinus' usual level of argument, however, and reveals either prejudice or political motives. One cannot deny that things change their properties according to their relations. He could with as much reason have maintained that one should not expect the sun to give any more heat at noonday than at sunrise, or that objects should look the same from all angles and distances.

There then follows a doctrinal objection to the apparent pluralism which would make the planets independent sources of power, acting arbitrarily. Plotinus holds that whatever power they may have, they are all subject to that of the First Cause, and it is at this point that he partially reverses the scientific point of view followed so far. It is just because all things proceed from one Cause that all different realms should be coordinated with one another. The Whole is manifest in each part, as there is but one Model for all. This idea of the unity of the world enables him then to accept the possibility that the planetary positions could serve as indicators of events on earth, while having no power to cause them. A common quality would pervade all things at each given moment, by which one part of the world should reveal something about other parts: "All teems with symbol; the wise man is the man who in any one thing can read another. . . ."[19] This idea is much the same as that of Synchronicity, which has gained ground in modern times. Coincidences may be uncaused in having no efficient causes, while some more subtle connection is at work instead.

The oneness of all things, besides requiring a common Source, requires a margin of qualitative correspondence between each being and those proximate to it, as already discussed in connection with magical attraction. Though any being may differ completely from others beyond those it is directly related to, the correspondence between all proximate parts ensures the cohesion of the world, and therewith all the synchronicities, which may have formal, though not efficient, causes. But by making the stars indicators of causality rather than causes in themselves, one does not alter the fact that one has admitted an all-embracing causality, which would seem to threaten what has been argued for free will. As if aware of this, he states at the beginning of the next passage:

> Soul, then, in the same way, is intent upon a task of its own; in everything it does it counts as an independent source of motion; . . . but a law of justice goes with every action in the Universe which, otherwise, would be dissolved, and is perdurable because the entire fabric is guided as much by the orderliness as by the power of the controlling force.[20]

The implication is that the power of free will and the controlling power of necessity exist side by side, with neither able to abolish the other, and also that freedom's activity is by nature partly within, and partly outside, the realm of necessity. This could be expressed by saying that we have a realm where we can make choices, and another in which we can *choose the choices*. On the one hand, there is the will's limited freedom in the external, and on the other, the order of intelligible reality, and therewith a higher or extra-phenomenal choice as to how much of our activity should be directed

19. *Enn.* ii, 3, 7.
20. *Enn.* ii, 3, 8.

to either. The content of the choice "before birth" would seem to be comprehended by some such reality, in view of the subsistent reality of the intelligibles, to which the mind can relate as much as to material things.

Choosing the Choice

This can be linked to the three criteria of free will, in that the first two, those of causal efficacy and circumstantial knowledge, belong to what has just been referred to as the external realm of choice, while the third, that of orientation to values, belongs to the higher choice-of-choices. The latter is evidently what is essential to the "emancipated" life, the loss of which deprives the will of its extra-phenomenal power of choice, and leaves it

> fate-bound, no longer profiting, merely, by the significance of the sidereal system, but becoming as it were a part and sunken in it, and dragged along with the whole thus adopted.[21]

Freedom can therefore be possessed in innumerable different degrees, depending on the balance between the phenomenal and extra-phenomenal directions. It is never lost absolutely, and its normative function is twofold, that of being a counter-realm to that of physical necessity, and that of being the means whereby the individual reorientates himself so as to enter it more fully, extricating himself from a passive relation to natural causality. But the failure of its operation is nevertheless possible, in which case the individual will remain a more or less undifferentiated part of the macrocosm, and not develop into a microcosm.

There is however, a possible objection to this conception of the will, which is purely a deduction from Plotinus, and not stated directly by him. The option of choosing the domain in which choice is to be made, and the nature of the choices there, could give rise to an infinite regress. An answer to this can be found in an inherent distinction among infinite regresses themselves, which arises between those which could be called vicious because they form a

---

21. *Enn.* ii, 3, 9.

real barrier between the things one is trying to relate, and those which could be called neutral or benign, because they result only *a posteriori* from the connection of the realities in question. In the present instance, it may be admitted that in choosing the choice we are implicitly also choosing-to-choose the choice, and so on, but this could still be acceptable, provided that the required relation does not lie at the far end of the regress.

An example of the vicious infinite regress is to be found in a criticism of Locke's theory of Representationalism, whereby an object becomes known through a representation of it being formed in the mind. But the representation itself is another kind of object, whence the problem of knowing it is essentially the same as that of knowing the original object, with the result that it must in turn be made the subject of a representation. That gives rise to the need for a third representation, and so on, from which it appears that knowledge never can be reached in this way, no matter how many representations are formed. Here, the regress would truly bar the way between the object and the knowledge of it, the object being known by mental representation.

Another such example is in the attempt to explain personal identity by reincarnation, that is, by its transfer from one person to another. If the identity we know as Peter is really that of Paul from a previous life, we cannot rest there with our answer, because by the same token Paul must in turn be simply the transfer of a yet earlier person, say, John. John likewise recedes into another predecessor, whence the required explanation of Peter's identity is removed to infinity. This regress also is vicious because the identities we want to relate lie at opposite ends of it.

However, the regress involved by choosing the choice is not of this kind, since it resembles the way in which the statement "I know A" gives rise to: "I know that I know A," and so on. It can be seen that the latter regress develops, not from one of its terms separately, but from their original conjunction, so that the latter is not broken by the regress that follows from it. Figuratively speaking, the vicious infinite regress would develop along a straight line between the basic terms, while the other kind would develop along a loop which connects with the junction of the two terms.

50

Another example of the benign infinite regress is to be seen in the case of an artist who completes his picture of a landscape with a rear view of himself painting it in the foreground, where the picture painted by the self-portrait contains yet another such picture of him, and so on. The relation of landscape to canvas proceeds only through the artist, and not through the regress, which is only a by-product of this relation. Similarly, there is the related case in optics, where one may hold up a second mirror to one's reflection in the first mirror, and see what is in principle an infinite series of images-of-images of oneself. Here it is quite clear that the cause of the regress is the relation between oneself and one's first image, and that nothing depends on the regress.

The will's complex power of choice frees Providence from responsibility for the actions of individuals, and also does so because the system of cosmic influences and "magical" attractions and repulsions does not reach into the rational center of the will. Humanity is said to be "poised midway between Gods and beasts,"[22] and so is moved now toward the one and now toward the other. This is important in regard to free will, as the outward or cosmic position of mankind would thus reflect the inward structure of the individual, as described according to the *Timaeus* at the end of Chapter 1. Man completes the chain of being by constituting the connecting link between higher and lower orders of being, without being intrinsically assimilated to either. This position defines three basic possibilities, one of growing more like the Gods, another of growing more like the beasts, and the more common one of remaining somewhere in between.

Plotinus' system is thus highly voluntaristic, with many things resulting from human wills that are not usually thought to do so. In this way the problem of evil is much reduced, and even where evil is most undeniably evident, it can still be considered limited by the compensatory negligence principle. Running through Plotinus' thought is the idea that, as man is in a central state and has the power in his will to attain higher states, many of his misfortunes are

---

22. *Enn.* III, 2, 8.

in a real sense self-inflicted through his failure to cultivate this possibility. It is an evil that the strong should oppress the weak, but he has no difficulty in showing that the only alternative would be even worse, since the oppression results simply from the law of cause and effect. The only natural alternative would in effect mean a chaos in which no result could be relied on to be produced by any faculty; nothing can be gained from giving up causality.

The same thinking is applied to man's relations with the Gods, since it is said that man cannot expect divine protection when he lives in ways that have no relation to what the Gods require of him. Their response depends on the extent of man's share in their nature, in accordance with a basic condition for causality. There is a parallel here with Judaism, as the Old Testament's most recurrent theme is that natural evils result from failure to obey the Commandments.

The onset of wrongs and disorders is the manifestation of a more universal order, therefore, and if man did not suffer evils while living in a deluded manner, the resulting disorder would be even more profound. Up till recent times, the thinking of literate Christians has not differed much from this position, either. For example, a Catholic philosopher such as Joseph de Maistre could say in so many words that human evils were the results of sins against the Commandments.

Where applications to politics are considered, the same approach is used by Plotinus to modify our attitude to misrule, as the rule of bad men is blamed on the feebleness or carelessness of the ruled. One may assume that Plotinus would have endorsed the saying that every country gets the government it deserves. The existence of evils is not only consistent with Providence, but is the price of the possibility of an effective collaboration with it, while man is always free to act against it.

The question as to whether evil might be involuntary is briefly considered, (*Enn.* III, 2, 10) but the existence of any necessity for us to be evil is ruled out in the light of all that has been said in regard to man's being inherently a causal agent. However, the inevitability of evil in general is accepted, and is illustrated by a comparison with the painting of a picture, in which dark colors are just as necessary for the finished whole as light ones. To complain of the existence of evil human beings is also said to be like complaining that not all the characters in a play are heroes. Every degree of good is in some sense a warrant for some other less than itself; here, as elsewhere, he makes a direct appeal to what is called the Principle of Plenitude by A.O. Lovejoy in *The Great Chain of Being*. Plotinus' thought is steeped in the metaphysic expounded in Lovejoy's book, which accounts for its cool and tolerant quality, combined nevertheless with a robust spiritual optimism.[23]

But the inevitability of wrongdoing in the world is never taken to excuse it, however. (The Gospels also state that evils must needs come, while condemning those by whom they come.) Human agency may or may not do things which, in themselves, are part of the world-order for good or ill, without anyone being compelled so to act, rather as the fact that a given number of road accidents will certainly happen in a given time does not necessitate any one individual to be involved in one.

The life of an individual is also compared with the role of an actor, not in the sense of its being equated with the role, but in the sense of its being imposed upon an intrinsic character, which must begin to work out its purposes for good or ill within the role's possibilities. The choice-of-choice principle implies that life's roles can be transcended, and can even be ultimately expendable.[24]

Complementary to our position between higher and lower realities, our freedom is also based on the composite nature of our inward being, which embraces things as varied as the vegetal, animal, and rational principles. (*Enn.* iii, 4, 2) The nature of each individual is decided by the direction of his life, which in turn is a function of whichever of the component principles is the one most intensely lived. For this reason, man must "break away towards the High," that is, towards the Intellectual-Principle and God. We are therefore said to have a range of equally possible identities, and for

---

23. Principle of Plenitude clearly stated, *Enn.* ii, 9, 3. Also Proclus, E.T. props. 26–29.

24. This dual nature of the will's function is also reflected in Kant's philosophy, with his distinction between *Wille* (Noumenal choice?) and *Willkur*. He was not directly influenced by Plotinus, so here again a universal conception emerges.

this reason we must discern and strive for whichever of them comprises the fullest reality.

The assumption is that "oneself" is defined by the mode of operation of the will, which is conceived as being able to deploy its energies in conjunction with any one of the basic principles which make up human beings. This ignores the personal aspect of identity, but it is an important truth, aspectually speaking:

> For the soul is many things . . . and each of us is an intellectual cosmos, linked to the world by what is lowest in us, but, by what is highest, to the Divine Intellect. (*Enn.* III, 4, 3)

Each human life is said to be attended by a tutelary spirit, which is "the power which consummates the chosen life," but it does not take over the power of choice from the soul, and is by no means a part of the soul, as both the life and the tutelary spirit are chosen in the extra-temporal state, as in *Republic* X. Plotinus also follows Plato's explanation in the *Timaeus* as to why the soul fails to be governed by its higher phase. The disturbance it suffers from birth is what disorganizes it, and this initial misdirection of its energies, even when corrected, can go on having effects throughout life. The connection with the doctrine of Original Sin can be seen here.

The Basis of Choice: the "Conjoint"

The causal account of the soul's liberation is said to be its taking up into itself its own lower phase, whose natural function is to be distributed within the sensible realm. This change renders the relation to a tutelary spirit unnecessary. This lower psychic phase (the conjoint principle) is the one which is instrumental in the union of body and soul, (*Enn.* II, 3,9) its experiences being also those of the personal soul. Its function is according to the Platonic principle of joining unlike things by median entities, which partake of the properties of both of them.

What is in question is an elaborate system of dualities, but one which was not pursued as an extension of science, or even of purely theoretical knowledge. While it comprises these elements, it was also a system of self-development, though one in which theory had a part to play. The importance of dualities here is that development presupposes widely differing states, which are nevertheless closely enough related for there to be communication between them. When distinguished according to value, they serve as benchmarks in relation to which development could be judged.

Thus the distinction of body and soul, with its idea of the interplay of different realities, adds a dynamic, developmental and therefore mystically effectual dimension to the task of theorizing. The study of the theoretical scheme involved in this is taken to be an incentive to the self development aspect, rather as though what religion understands as the salvation of the soul could be made the subject of a kind of natural history which confirmed it. This would explain why Platonism has historically proved acceptable to Christians, Moslems, Buddhists, and Jews, as well as to those who hold a belief in divinity without having any specific religion. It all relates to something too close to the inner workings of the spiritual life for it to be able to come into conflict with any of the particular doctrines, values, or practices, on which religions are based.

Much of man's motivation is said not to reside in either the body or soul *per se*, but in the "conjoint" or "couplement". The soul's higher freedom can be seen from the point of view of its being able to choose how far it lives to the conjoint principle, and how far to its unmingled state. Insofar as it lives to the conjoint principle, its reason-principle becomes weakened, although sharing in the compromise nature peculiar to the median reality, where it must in any case compete with many more things which can engage the will equally.

Related to this, it is maintained that pleasure and pain do not pertain to either body or soul as such, but only to their intermediary. The body as such cannot suffer, even from its own dissolution, while the soul cannot undergo any such thing, whereas the conjoint can and does undergo dissolution. The will is also referred to as the "mid-point", not because of some quasi-spatial setting, but as a focal point of action:

But does not the We include that phase of our being which stands above the mid-point? It does, but on condition that we lay hold of it: our entire nature is not ours at all times, but only as we direct the mid-point upwards or downwards, or lead some particular phase of our nature from potentiality or native character into act. (*Enn.* I, 1, 11)

Here is the Plotinian basis of free will, precisely. This freedom of movement of the will's focus is however subject to the limitation referred to above, in regard to the weakening of the reason-principle by its involvement with the conjoint. While the transfer of the focus of voluntary action from one part of the personality to another is always free in principle, it requires the co-operation of reason, failing which, its changes would be practically random, and so not free at all. But the more the voluntary focal point is bound to sense and opinion, the more the reasoning power will be either stifled or deprived of its full range of application. For this reason, the will's theoretical freedom can in practice be compromised by the direction in which it is employed. This seems to follow from the premises (a) that the will can transfer itself according to the dictates of reason, and (b) that one of the two states between which it acts is one where reason acts unhindered, while the other is one where reason is but one voice amid many others. This can also be taken as a metaphysical commentary on what Aristotle says in Book III of the *Ethics*, where he briefly examines the possibility that at least some uses of the free will have the effect of leading it into a state of determination.

All physical pleasures and pains, desires and aversions, belong to the conjoint or couplement, it is maintained, on the grounds that there have to be "two phases of desire". (*Enn.* IV, 4, 20). There are chronologically prior, but very ill-formed desires in the body, which are followed by corresponding states in the conjoint phase which "reads" and then "enhances" them, so to speak, to work them up into articulate desires, unless the will rules that, when read, they should be either denied or postponed. These divisions within our interior life are also held to be objective and necessary because of two facts, firstly the constant impact of pleasures, pains, illnesses, and stresses of various kinds, and secondly the clear consciousness we have of these things, which is not in itself disordered by them.

Thus the soul, or at least its rational phase, is not affected by what we take to be the soul's distresses. The perception of a distress is not itself a distress, and must be immune from it, if it is to register the distress correctly:

> a messenger, affected, overwhelmed by the event, would either not convey the message or not convey it faithfully (*Enn.* IV, 4, 19).

This gives special emphasis to a deep difference among inward states, the moved and the immovable. The will thereby has the choice of adhering more to the conscious activity which is a spectator to the disturbances of the sensible world, or to involve itself more deeply in the latter. The freedom of choice in regard to externals depends thus on a freedom of choice among powers of the soul, which is conceived as an epitome of all it relates to outwardly.

Pure Intellect and Human Intellect

The world of natural phenomena reflects in its own way what Plotinus says of the soul. Peaceful and orderly scenes are perceptible because light travels in straight lines, and its angles of incidence and reflection are equal, while sound waves are propagated by corresponding laws. When, on the other hand, we perceive scenes of confusion and violence, it is only because light and sound continue to be propagated in exactly the same manner. Even the grossest alternations of order and disorder therefore do not make the least difference to the underlying order of natural laws on which all the events are based. This distinction between a substratum of constant order, both in nature and in the soul, contrasting with a realm in which infinitely varied things can happen without any regard to order, reveals something of the relation between freedom and determination. It shows again from yet another angle, that these two things are intrinsically opposites, even though inseparable, and that the determination to which material things are subject is a necessary condition for the freedom of other beings.

But this may seem inconsistent with Plotinus' idea that freedom lies in voluntary identification with the constant and unaffected soul-phase, and not with the sense-oriented one, though in fact this only shows that the analogy with natural phenomena must not be pressed too far. This is because the unity of the person is far from being impaired by what might be taken for a one-sided identification with the reason-principle. Such it would be, if the corporeal and sensible phases were objectively or physically separable from the intellectual phase. By the *eidos*-instance relation, the lower or more individual phases of our being contain only what is implicit in the intellectual phase. Therefore, the identification with the intellect really serves to integrate the whole personality, and not to get rid of part of it.

Consequently, the attachment of the will to the intellect joins it to a realm of possibilities which is in principle richer, and from whence it can most readily extend its action to others. Thus it is only superficially a paradox that freedom should be associated with a state which is outside the sphere of activities in which freedom is normally understood to be enjoyed.

The state of full freedom for Plotinus, as opposed to common sense, necessarily goes beyond the range of the sensory, emotive, and imaginative faculties, whence it is unable to claim our attention by creating a subjective clamor as they can. Its apparent emptiness is only an emptiness for sense and imagination, of course, but as sense defines the usual point of view, the terminology of emptiness is often used for this kind of reality. Examples of this are plentiful in Eastern teachings, as in the Tao Te Ching, with its frequent references to this kind of emptiness. The penalty, in terms of freedom, for ignoring the "empty" aspect of the soul-life is by no means immediately evident, but it inevitably leads to relations with alien wills and forces in which one's own will has less and less control or relevance.

As for general criticism of this philosophy, I have postponed it as much as possible, because Plotinian thought contains a doctrine of human life in which the intelligence is rated at its true value, and which is too little heard today. But Plotinus, and Neoplatonism generally, is open to at least one fundamental criticism which, while not falsifying it, requires that its scope must have certain limits. This follows from its own general premise that man is the Little World, as the world is the Great Man; man therefore has some part of his being which corresponds to universal Reality, through which he is able to know the universal. If he can thus know the All, what need has he for any other wisdom or provision for personal life? Following this approach, Neoplatonism could well merge with Buddhism and Advaita Vedanta, which do not recognize personal identity.

But here, just where all seems most assured, there arises an eternal paradox, namely, that knowledge of the All arises from the intellectual faculties of individual persons, not from universals. Thus an exclusive development towards pure intellect could only mean an attempt to equate the whole person with what remains by definition one of his own powers or faculties. What man calls his "intellect" is not the Intellect or Nous as such, but the part or faculty of the soul which is able to interact directly with Intellect. If the soul's intellectual faculty was Intellect itself, error would be impossible and disincarnate spirituality would be perfectly valid. Given, however, that the human state manifests an eternal form and is not a mere aggregate of items among which the Intellect happens to be included, our essential need is for a wisdom of the whole person such as it has been historically the role of Christianity to provide. This is an issue to which Plotinus gives too little attention, for all the merits of his conception of free will. Fortunately, Platonism is sufficiently flexible to allow personalist as well as impersonalist readings.

3

Alexander and the Denial of Necessity

An Opponent of Stoicism

Alexander of Aphrodisias lived during the second half of the Second and the first half of the Third century AD. Little is known of his life, but it is known that he was appointed by Marcus Aurelius to teach Platonic, Aristotelian, and Epicurean philosophy at Athens in AD 176. That he continued in this official position is indicated by the fact that his work *On Fate* was dedicated to the emperors Septimius Severus and Caracalla, and this is what dates it between AD 198 and 209. Of the commentators on Aristotle, he is the earliest from whom a substantial amount of writings survives, and he is also important as the last of the Peripatetics, while he lived just at the beginning of the period of the Neoplatonists. He was not head of the Lyceum, however, because that had ceased to exist in 86 BC, but his interpretations of Aristotle were accepted by his contemporaries as authoritative, from which he came to be called "the Commentator".

On Fate is directed entirely against the idea that all things are necessitated, as they would be according to the arguments of the Stoics. A number of these arguments are stated, but there is no mention of their authors, rather as though they were common currency at the time. His arguments against them are thoroughly Aristotelian, and there are the same appeals to common sense as are found in Aristotle, though sometimes he has to go well beyond common sense. Nevertheless, his general tendency is shown by the general argument that nature does nothing in vain, and that it is natural to feel regret at making mistakes, which would make no sense if we erred by necessity.

Alexander and the Denial of Necessity

Aristotle is generally favorable to free will, and Alexander develops this tendency as far as he can. His denial of necessity went even further than that of the Platonists, who maintained that fate or necessity prevailed in a sphere of its own, and that beings not naturally part of it could be drawn into it or escape from it. As the word "fate" will be frequently used, it should be noted that it is used only as it appears in Alexander's text, an archaic equivalent of causal necessity, unconnected with the romantic idea of some alien will mysteriously invading one's own.

In one place[1] he argues against universal causality on the grounds that the idea contains something contradictory, rather after the manner of the Thesis in Kant's Third Antinomy. If there was nothing but cause and effect, their series would extend to infinity, so ruling out a First Cause. This would subvert causality itself, as it is dependent on objective termini to define its activity. Further on, it is also argued in the same manner[2] that if everything had to have a cause, these causes themselves would all be effects, and therefore just as much in need of explanation as the things which those causes explained. Thus nothing would truly be a source, whether of action or of knowledge.

His alternative is to make an exception to the rule of causality, and make all causes depend on a cause which itself has no cause. To this is joined all that is actually happening, by way of a number of causes and effects which is finite, no matter how large. In this way, the causal principle is saved, though at the price of its universality. It is argued in the same place that if knowledge is what pertains to first causes, the extension of causal series to infinity would extinguish knowledge as well as causality. When we say that knowledge is of the causes of things, what we have in mind are causes which stand out from the crowd, so to speak, and have the role of sources in relation to others. But this kind of cause would be logically untenable unless causal series were finite. When philosophers say that such-and-such has a cause, they are not concerned to affiliate it to something else with no more causal power than it has. But if the causal series were

1. *On Fate,* xxv.
2. Ibid., Mantissa, xxii, 169.

infinite there would be no other order of causality, and our natural conviction as to the reality of causal knowledge would be confuted. Alexander's argument rests on the validity of this natural conviction.

If there is an archetypal Uncaused Cause, there would seem to be nothing in the idea of it to compel it to be unique *qua* uncaused. As its existence also would establish the general possibility of such a cause, there would then be no reason why there may not be many other, lesser kinds of uncaused causes, even in the midst of a world ruled in general by causality. A Platonist would say that the uncaused First Cause was the *eidos* of these uncaused causes, though there is no such expression in Alexander.

Uncaused Events

In the Mantissa to *On Fate*,[3] Aristotle's *Metaphysics* is quoted in defense of the idea that there can be uncaused events, because in this passage, Aristotle contends that there can be no science of the accidental *per se*, because knowledge relates only to what either always is or usually is, whereas the accidental is neither of these things. The conclusion is that if there is no science of the accidental, it cannot arise from the causes which are the subject of knowledge, whence it cannot be truly a real thing. Aristotle expresses the matter as follows:

> for accidental being is apparently something akin to non-being. And this is clear also from arguments such as this: any other type of being undergoes generation and destruction, but accidental being does not.[4]

Here Aristotle follows Plato in directly equating the real with the knowable. This also highlights the distinction between logic and ontology, as for the former everything is sharply divided between "is" and "is not", whereas ontology has no such clear limits for being, because the principle that distinct realities are joined by mean ones which partake something of both applies to both being

3. XXII, 170.1, 10.
4. *Metaphysics*, 1026b, 20.

and non-being. There can thus be a being permeated with non-being, and therewith the uncaused. This idea is further supported by the distinction between eternal things and those which perish. The perishable owes its nature to its admixture of non-being, which leaves it open to the action of destructive forces which break up whatever it has of being, rather as a damaged part of an apple is a center from which the whole fruit will go bad eventually.

This theory has also a connection with Plato inasmuch as the possibility of a real non-being is the subject of the *Sophist*. An imitation of a reality is said to be only "like" it:

> *Str*: Then by what is 'like' you mean what has not real existence, if you are going to call it "not real". *Theaet*: But it has some sort of existence. *Str*: Only not real existence, according to you. *Theaet*: No; except that it really is a likeness. *Str*: So, not having real existence, it really is what we call a likeness? *Theaet*: Real and unreal do seem to be combined in that perplexing way, and very queer it is. *Str*: Queer indeed. You see that now again by dovetailing them together in this way our hydra-headed Sophist has forced us against our will to admit that "what is not" has some sort of being.[5]

There is also an implicit Platonic aspect to this idea which comes from the *eidos*-instance relation. If all the instances of the *eide* actually formed a continuum, the total result would hardly differ from another *eidos*, whereas in reality, the forms or *eide* are constantly entering and vacating something which is not adequate to retain them and can hold their manifestations only unstably. This conception of the material world makes the idea of its being permeated with void parts follow almost *a priori*. On this basis, Alexander argues[6] that the only things that really depend on us are those of which we could just as easily bring about the opposite. However, if we can effect opposite things, their cause in us must be capable of producing *contrary effects*. But this contradicts the idea of natural

---

5. *Sophist*, 240b–c.
6. *Mantissa*, 173.1, 10.

causality. Therefore our (free) actions would have to be causeless from a scientific point of view.

This is why he extends what Plato and Aristotle have said about non-being so that there may be "some motion without a cause", which is thought to suffice for the phenomenon he has in mind. What he calls "*per accidens* being" is a kind of not-being which attaches to practically everything, and constitutes what he calls the "slackness and weakness", which infects everything in nature. Consciousness of this "privation" in his own makeup is said to be the cause of man's desire for the good by which he may escape the consequences of this deficiency.

Allied to this is the idea that there are degrees of being and reality, which conflicts with the more common sense idea that things either are or are not. A greater range of possibilities will be realized if there are many degrees of being, as opposed to a fixed quantity of it in everything. Also, this proposed variability in degrees of being would fit well with the idea that progressive changes in things lead them finally to pass the barriers from existence to non-existence, and vice-versa. The discontinuous change would then be the culmination of a continuous process oriented towards it. In one sense, a symphony does not exist until it is finished, but there is also a real sense in which it gradually "exists more" as it goes towards completion. A human being could be said to exist more, or less, depending on whether his state of health tended away from, or towards death.

The "cause *per accidens*", then, does not exist specifically for what it brings about. If it does effect something in the external world, the event is attributed to the fortuitous and luck, whereas if it operates within us, it is the ground of our free will, since it can only mean that certain things must depend on ourselves alone. We do not always react in the same way to the same situations. This is due to the presence in us of the "weakness and slackness" of not-being already referred to. We should note that freedom is not the word for the variations in our behavior which derive only from this source, since it is only indetermination. Uniform responses imply a mastery over external conditions, and therefore both a more substantial freedom and a causal power.

Two kinds of things are said to depend on us. One is due to

nature, training, and habit, and in this case our relation to what is done is more like that of a cause in the normal sense of the word. The other is the causeless kind, which is related to the mixture of not-being which interrupts the continuity of the causal flow in us. But this is the vindication of free will which has just been said to be compromised by its being dependent on something purely negative, made possible only by the presence of weakness and deficiency.

This view is countered in Mantissa XXIII,[7] where man is said to be the most honourable being in the world because his actions alone can be the result of deliberation, which may or may not allow them. This power of deliberation deploys itself through the discontinuities made by the causeless condition. The latter condition could be envisaged on different levels. On the natural level, it could simply be due to the absence of anything sufficiently effective among causes to bring any one of them into play, whereas on the level of the Plotinian conception of free will, it would be due to the operation of mind and will in a realm outside the one in which natural causes can function. These two aspects could well be complementary, as the interaction between an intellect transcending natural causes, and a natural order with numerous causal hiatuses in it, would fit the conception of causality in broken sequences proposed in Chapter 1 to resolve the antinomy between causal absolutism and lawlessness.

Man's will is said to be the beginning or origin of his actions, and as such cannot have an external cause.[8] If we supposed it did have such a cause, that cause would constitute a "beginning of the beginning" which would be meaningless. Whatever has its point of departure in us can by definition have no other cause anywhere else, and if the will has its share of causelessness in some of its movements, through the weakness of not-being, its relation to the intellectual-principle nevertheless prevents it from being wholly passive. The act of deliberation, which is taken as the manifestation of free will (not named as such) is seen to consist in man's ability to see

7. Alexander, *On Fate*, Mantissa, 173.1, 10–35; 174.1, 1–10.
8. That is to say, no cause in the natural sense, which is compatible with its being brought into existence by creation.

through appearances to some more significant reality, and this is not shared by any other creature.

As Alexander conceives free will in terms of a compound of an active principle (deliberation) and passive principle (causelessness), so he conceives the user of free action as a *compound cause* consisting of the deliberation; the choice; the decision; and the man. This is a fuller view of the deliberating force, which steps into the breach wherever there is causelessness. Being a compound, it is not bound always to produce the same effect under the same conditions like a true natural cause, whence it could give rise to a positive inconsistency more in keeping with free will than negative inconsistency, though the two may be hard to distinguish from without. Positive inconsistency is accounted for by the fact that one's attention is usually divided successively among a variety of goals to be achieved, while the best means to even one such end are seen to vary with changing circumstances.

This reasoning is clearly related to Aristotle's *Ethics*, as also where it is argued that deliberation is valid because it is natural, and because nature never does anything in vain. As we do not deliberate about past or eternal things, what we do deliberate about proves we know a class of things which really are in our power.[9] Another important argument is based on the fact that we all believe it possible to act in error,[10] whereas if fate ruled everything, error would not only be impossible, the very idea of it would be without meaning.

Another argument concerns the unity of the universe.[11] The fatalists maintain that all things must be rigorously connected, because otherwise the Universe would belie its name. Thus any causeless motion would have no connection with anything before it, and then there would only be a multitude of more or less unrelated fragments which could not strictly be "a" or "one" multitude at all.

Alexander tries to refute this, but not very effectively, on the grounds that there are all kinds of being which produce no effects: humans and animals with no offspring; deformities of the body;

---

9. Mantissa, 178.8–181.1.
10. Ibid., 191.2–191.25.
11. *On Fate*, 191.2–193.3.

plants that die before they are grown up. This argument is too superficial and popular; no being can be called causeless, or without causality, just because it fails to produce the effect that beings of its type most typically produce. In fact everything has effects which are quite extraneous to its formal purpose and nature, and it is curious that Alexander should have ignored this fact in this connection, as the role of the "cause *per accidens*" forms an important part of his theory. As for the unity of the universe, that would seem to consist more in the manifestation of form than in the mere mechanical connection of separate parts.

Causality, Sequence, and Coincidence

We are on firmer ground with the next argument,[12] that causal necessity is a one-way thing: if Socrates is to exist, it is necessary that his father must first have existed; but conversely, this does not imply that the existence of his father made that of Socrates necessary. This at least shows that causality does not bind all things together in the same way, as determinism would assert. In the same place, he proceeds to an idea which anticipates Hume, where he makes the point that constant succession, like that of day and night, or standing up and walking, do not mean that one has caused the other, even though a single cause may embrace them both, as the earth's rotation does day and night. (Hume's reasoning deliberately discounts this distinction between succession and causality.)

But manifestly the Isthmian Games are not caused by the Olympian, nor Winter by Summer, and we are clear about the reason why. Consequently the realm of causality has clear boundaries, as there are classes of regular events which do not owe their connections to it, and others in which causal connection is binding in one sense only.

Alexander also instances reason as evidence for freedom, because a rationally contrived action depends on one's ability to choose it. The same interpretation is made by Boethius,[13] where he shows that

12. Ibid., 194.1–195.1.
13. *De Consol. v*, 11.

reason cannot be present in us without the power of judgment, and that judgment can do nothing unless it can freely choose some things and reject others. But we know which things happen through reason, such as the making of artifacts, as opposed to those which simply come about by nature. Consequently reason, or the ability to act in accordance with it, ensures freedom, or in Alexander's terms, ensures that one's fate does not bind one by necessity. This relation between freedom and reason is also essential in Kant's theory of ethics:

> A rational being belongs as a *member* to the kingdom of ends when, although giving universal laws in it, he is also himself subject to these laws. He belongs to it *as sovereign* when, while giving laws, he is not subject to the will of any other. A rational being must always regard himself as giving laws...in a kingdom of ends which is rendered possible by the freedom of the will.[14]

Reason necessarily confronts us with real options, for the sake of which the will must be free. In regard to the idea that everything comes about by necessity, the absurdity of saying that a thing like a bed or a house came into being by fate is pointed out[15] in view of the fact that such things are made according to rational principles by those who, being rational, must also have the freedom to make them. The only things which can be said to come about by fate are those which happen by nature, and this leads Alexander to an effective identification of nature with fate:

> For what is fated is in accordance with nature, and what is in accordance with nature is fated. For it is not the case that man comes to be from man, and horse from horse, in accordance with nature, but not in accordance with fate; rather these causes accompany each other as if differing only in name.[16]

However, the productions of reason and nature have this much in common, that they both occur for the sake of something else, as

---

14. *Groundwork to the Metaphysic of Morals,* 433–434.
15. *On Fate,* 169.1, 5–10.
16. Ibid., 169.1, 20.

opposed to things which happen by luck or chance. But even here, Alexander denies that fate always implies necessity:

[The] coming to be of the things that come to be in this way is sometimes hindered.[17]

Here he argues that if, as is generally conceded, things can happen contrary to nature, they must also happen contrary to fate, in view of the identification made between them. In this reasoning, the common sense ideas of the natural and the unnatural are accepted uncritically. Nature or fate, then, is the compendium of ideal patterns, which have varying degrees of force behind them, but which are never absolute.

An important argument for uncaused events is based on there being accidental or lucky happenings, which result from a cause which was designed for an entirely different effect. Causes have what we might call an element of "causal leakage", whereby their activity extends unintentionally to things quite unrelated to them. Such is the import of the "cause *per accidens*". The familiar example of this is the act of digging to cultivate a garden, which leads to the discovery of a treasure buried there. This also illustrates the idea that a cause having uniformly the same effect cannot rule out its producing totally irregular effects at the same time, depending on circumstances.

The assertion that all things happen by necessity, however, would do away with the distinction between regularly-caused and lucky events. But this distinction is clearly evident, as in the case where treasure was dug up while one was digging for something else, as compared with the case where treasure was dug up after someone set out to find it. Here again, a universally accepted notion is appealed to. The lucky event is said to have no cause, although this really means that it has no cause *per se* known to us, and no cause connected with our own choice of activity.

This question of lucky events or coincidences having no causes has been taken up in recent years by R. Sorabji,[18] in connection

17. Ibid., 169.1, 30.
18. *Necessity, Cause and Blame*, chap. 1.

with two obscure passages in Aristotle's *Metaphysics*,[19] where he evidently intends to deny that everything happens by necessity. With some amplification, these passages can be taken to be an argument against universal necessity on the grounds that there is at least one class of events, namely coincidences, for which there need be no causes. According to Sorabji, Alexander implicitly follows and develops Aristotle's denial that coincidences need have any causes.

The example given here by Aristotle is that of a man who eats something which makes him thirsty, which causes him to go out to the well to get some water. Meanwhile, some other series of causes has caused some ruffians to be at the well at the same time, as a result of which, the man who goes there gets murdered. This murder is simply the result of a coincidence between arrivals at the well, and, as such, requires no cause outside the separate series of causes which brought each of the protagonists there. This would certainly agree with the scientific principle of the economy of hypotheses, but as this is really a guide as to how knowledge should be handled, rather than a truth as to how the world actually is, some further reason needs to be given.

Had there been no coincidence, and a period of a few hours had elapsed between these arrivals at the well, we should be entirely satisfied with the separate causal sequences which led to each arrival. When events happen serially like this, no one ever thinks of asking for reasons for the time interval between them, so long as no kind of plot is in question. Cases of coincidence are viewed differently, however, mainly because they affect our personal interests, but this should not affect our understanding of the theory. If we re-define coincidences as members of serial events, between which the time interval happens to be zero, there would then be no more reason to seek a separate cause for the zero time in such cases, than for the random time intervals arising in serial cases generally.

This, I think, should suffice to confirm what has been said concerning the evident lack of any need for a cause for coincidences. The fact that such events always make a strong psychological impression is no reason for excluding them from the class of serial

19. *Metaphysics,* 1027a, 30–1027b, 10.

events, where this kind of causal problem does not arise. In regard to the treasure, then, the causes for its being hidden in a certain place, and the causes which made someone go digging there, would suffice for a full explanation of the lucky event. Accordingly, the idea that coincidences might still have causes which remain obscure to us, is relegated by Alexander to the realm of magic, where effects attributed to amulets may be treated in the same way.

So far, the question has been treated solely in the light of efficient causality, since that is the kind which governs sequences of events, but this does not extend to some of the interactions based on common ideal-forms discussed in Chapter 2. The same question can be transposed in Platonic terms to the question as to whether there must be ideal-forms of things which consist solely of mixtures, as does mud from earth and water. It may well seem that the mixing of the water and the earth should be an event peculiar only to the material world, but if this were the case it would imply that the material world had a range of possibilities which was in some respects wider than that of the forms. Such an idea would clash with the role of the forms as being the formal causes of all things in the world, however. One answer to this is to distinguish between the forms of "standard eidetic possibilities" and the "marginal detritus" of the eidetic order, as J.N. Findlay expresses it.[20]

While having no causes in the scientific or physical sense of the word, therefore, coincidences may yet be caused in the sense of instancing an ideal-form common to the persons or things so related, which according to Plotinus effectively does relate the instances of a form to one another, as outlined in Chapter 2. However, it is far from clear whether a formal causality of this kind has any direct control over the will, which is essentially concerned with efficient causality, so we can allow that coincidences have some kind of cause without introducing the kind of causality that could condition the will.

A coincidence consists in an intersection between two different causal series. Now there is nothing in the idea of either series to show us whether it should or should not coincide with the other.

20. *Plato: The Written & Unwritten Doctrines,* chap. v, v.

But we have as first principles that both series are developing within the same time series, and in a common region of space, wherein each can occupy any part except the one occupied by the other. Given this, and a large enough number of causal series, it is inevitable statistically that some pairs among them will intersect sooner or later, that is, produce spatially juxtaposed effects at a given time. For this, there need be no efficient cause, just as we do not need to find causes for individual collisions among the randomly-moving molecules of a gas. Coincidences may thus be said to exist *a priori*, given that all causal series can deploy themselves without restriction within the same finite space-time system.

Whether it is a question of collisions between molecules or of intersections between causal series, therefore, one can say that there is a cause for this kind of event in general, namely their being members of the same space-time system, but no cause for any one instance of it. Thus coincidences are subject only to a loose and general kind of causality. If they could be shown to have individual causes *per se*, the above reasoning would be invalidated, but conversely, if we accept that it is valid, the conclusion will be that individual coincidences not only do not have, but *cannot* have causes *per se*.

In the light of the above, it can be observed that causality does not by any means apply to all things either with equal force or in the same way. This lack of uniformity is important in regard to free will, which requires that causes arising from rational processes can supervene upon causes which are governed by physical forces. If physical causality were everywhere uniform in its application, there would be no occasion for it to be supplemented or redirected by any other agency.

The Reality of Non-Being

Before passing on to more general considerations, we need to refer again to Alexander's most metaphysical statement, that "there is not-being in the things that are, diffused somehow among them and accompanying them."[21] This is held to be the basis of uncaused

---

21. *On Fate*, Mantissa, 170.1, 10.

motion, necessary for the working of free will. In this connection he makes implicit use of Aristotle's idea of privation.[22] According to this idea the existence of all things in nature is said to involve privation, as a plant, for example, is said to be "deprived" of eyes, because each thing is found to be lacking in innumerable properties which belong to other things. Everything proclaims itself to be fragmentary on this basis. This has always been taken to explain why all things in nature are liable to change and decay. The privation of being is the means whereby both corruption and generation can take place. There can be no stability in things which never were complete by the absolute standard of having no privation, this affecting all material things. Theologians have traditionally used this idea to account for the corruption of fallen nature, and for nature's need to be sustained by divine power:

> Coetaneous with matter and form, privation is common to all creation. It is defect, the lack of that which should be present, "a kind of nothing". . . . When this potential force is set in motion, it disrupts the balances of nature and releases discords which eventually lead to dissolution.[23]

Also the possibility of error implies that non-being has some kind of reality, and therefore a share in beings, but above all this conception connects with the Platonic metaphysic of being, according to which *being does not exist*. If being is the ideal-form of existence, it clearly cannot be an existent itself, not through lack of reality, but an excess of it. Thus God is not an existent, on account of being principial Being ("I am").

But man, according to Plotinus, is composed from all levels of the real, these including the supra-existential realities of the Intellectual-Principle and the One. In Christian terms, this means that, while man is still a creature, a vital part of his being is above the created order of nature. It is accordingly "empty" or "void" in relation to the natural life; such is Plotinus' constant theme, only not so expressed, as he lacked the Biblical doctrine of creation.

22. *Metaphysics*, 1022b, 22–1023a.
23. V. Harris, *All Coherence Gone*, chap. 2, v.

The vital consequence of this is that, since God did not create the intellect, but rather delegated it to creatures, God cannot be supposed to have any power over it except to determine it to be what it must be, whence the uncreated or "supra-existent" intellect is the ultimate basis for freedom, as the "Unground" is for Jacob Boehme. To this it may be objected that it denies the divine omnipotence, though it only does so from the point of view of the simplistic idea of omnipotence referred to in Chapter 1. The best answer to this objection is that a God who creates beings with wills of their own, over which he has at least no direct control, is deploying a greater power than a God who produces creatures who are merely robotic projections of himself. (Calvinists and Orientalists in fact hold some such belief, but if God is the being than whom there can be none greater, they must be in difficulties.)

This conception is traditional, but during the Middle Ages there was a steady displacement of Platonic metaphysics by Aristotelian. One of the effects of this was the obscuration of the *eidos*-instance principle and its concomitant idea of the divine supra-existence by which alone God could be the principle of all existence. This led unintentionally to a conception of God as merely the Supreme Existent, creating all other existents with the ultimately transcendent (*hyperousios*) principle all but forgotten. But to be existent is to be determined, whence the creatures of a wholly determined being must themselves be wholly determined.

This was the doctrine of God-existent and man creature-entire which was taken at face value by Luther and Calvin, both of whom pursued it with perfect logic to the total denial of free will. Thus a crowning and systematic misconception grew out of centuries of deepening but haphazard misconception by theologians who had unwittingly lost sight of the distinction between Being and existence. This is partly explained by a relentless drift away from the spiritual pole of reality by the collective human mind with the passage of time, according to a cosmic principle which reflects the order of the descent of the creation itself. In human terms, it came about through the fact that the ideas of God having an inner life which transcends all that can be said of him as a person who creates, controls, and judges, and of man having in him an uncreated element, have never been welcome to those whose main concern is with the exoteric side of religion. The implied region of quasi-natural common ground between the human and the divine is seen to be inimical to the basic choices with which it is usually necessary to challenge the faith of the individual.

Thus a doctrine with the most potential for practical moral challenge is thereby preferred to metaphysical correctness, but the advantage gained in such ways always has to be paid for later, as history has shown. The Reformation doctrine slammed the door against metaphysical knowledge, and left Christian man a prisoner of his own mortality, from whence he could only hope to escape by an act of God. Yet it gained a mass following, because it offered a simplified religion, and one which allowed the individual more freedom (one cannot coerce a free will which is deemed not to exist). Thus attention was diverted from the metaphysical disaster, by the easing of matters of practice.

Although the full implications of the idea of the nonexistent in relation to freedom were not appreciated, Alexander was profoundly right to use it, but being an Aristotelian, he could not draw from it the symmetry of the non-existence which is beneath the existent because too unreal, and that which transcends it, through being the source of the real. This is the relation referred to already, between the transcendent nonexistent or supra-existent and the naturally non-existent. Both these opposed conceptions of real non-existences are unquestionably of Platonic origin, while Alexander's use of only one of them indicates an incomplete use of their metaphysical sources by the Aristotelians.

Given the paradoxical element of real non-existence in the world, Alexander proceeds directly from this to the idea of uncaused motion, without appearing to justify the conceptual leap involved in this. For his idea to be of use, it must be necessary for something in the category of the unreal to cause motion among the things which exist. But it is hard to see how the unreal could be said to act upon the real, as its unreality must imply a lack of causal power. Although Alexander does not appear to say so, this would really be a matter of a causal hiatus, which allows the intrusion of either a random natural cause, or that of a rational agent. In any case, it is clear that he associates the elements of not-being with the action of the cause *per accidens.*

Just as the accidental is only a fleeting and obscure part of the world, so also is the causality it gives rise to, inasmuch as it cannot be classified among the regular causes *per se.* Thus the unreal may be said to act upon the real in that it constitutes a boundary to the realm of necessary causality. Alexander does not make this point because he never draws the conclusion that causes *per se* constitute a realm of necessity in contradistinction to that of the causes *per accidens.* But if, as he sometimes seems to imply, there was no necessity anywhere except in arithmetic, there would be no need for him to establish the separate reality of the causes *per accidens,* as in fact he does.

This justifies criticisms of him on the grounds that he under-rates the principle of necessity in the world in his attempts to justify free will. But his deficiency in this regard does not invalidate his argument for specifically uncaused events. This argument is formed in three stages: firstly with Plato's conception of a reality between existence and non-existence; secondly with Aristotle's equation of this kind of quasi-existent with accidental phenomena,[24] and finally with Alexander's use of the accidental in the form of the cause *per accidens* as opposed to the cause *per se.* This kind of event is of the same kind as the one considered above where two causal series were said to intersect. When this intersection takes place, a causal agent in either series encounters something which never normally enters its sphere of operation. Thus the accidentality of the cause *per accidens* results from the accident whereby different causes *per se* enter adjacent portions of space at the same time.

Motivation in Broken Series

Relevant to this question of intersection of causal series is the idea of causality being a short-range phenomenon, as each series is sooner or later broken in upon by another. Instead of there being a set of parallel causal series extending from the beginning of the uni-verse to its end, there would be a multitude of quite short series

24. *Metaphysics,* 1026b–1027a.

in succession. The continuity of this system, and therefore of the world, is ensured by these series beginning and ending within the span of others. The life spans of all the creatures which inhabit a world exemplify this form of continuity.

If it is accepted that series of natural causes can and constantly do meet and terminate one another, the resulting element of accidentality gives grounds for acceptance of their also being interrupted by causal agents which are not natural forces, but are rational. The lack of homogeneity in the natural order implied by Alexander's idea of not-being pervading the world of being gives an additional reason for allowing the convergence of radically different kinds of causality:

> So what depends on us is a matter of that which through the existence of not-being has weakened the continuity of the causes in us; and it occupies this position, becoming a cause in cases where the necessary cause has failed on account of the mixing and interweaving of not-being in what is.[25]

This is the part of Alexander's account of free will which most tends to support the view of causality I have put forward already, and it is also closely dependent on the idea that being and reality admit of varying degrees. From being implicit in Plato, this conception has become traditional in Western thought where metaphysics is concerned. Aquinas is a source for its later development,[26] because his theology required that varying degrees of relation to God, the source of being, should be reflected in varying degrees of participation in being by all those so related.

Alexander also uses psychological arguments, as where he contends that a belief that everything is fated deprives mankind of any motive for exertion.[27] The less things are thought to depend on man's will, the more he will confine his activities to things which are easy and undemanding, and this will be manifest in a lowering of standards throughout a civilization, because labour is necessary for all kinds of excellence. Thus a change in the general belief about the

25. *On Fate*, Mantissa, 172.10–15.
26. SCG. II, 30, 6.
27. *De Fato*, 186.30–187.10.

freedom of the will can and does result in a visible change in the appearance of a society. Likewise moral standards would fall, because it must be a waste of time to correct the behavior of either oneself or of others, if everything comes about by necessity.

This is a more popular argument than the previous ones, but it makes the important point that what is believed about the will is causally effective enough to change the face of physical reality. The mere fact that there is any question of such outward changes shows that free will is in principle refutable, and thereby capable of confirmation from the scientific point of view. In a world which really was ruled by what is called fate in this context, on the other hand, changes in belief about the will would not change anything observable. The most morally objectionable aspect of hard determinism appears in the fact that belief in it takes away all meaning from both praise and blame, for which reason it works simultaneously against the interests of the morally good, and in favor of the wicked. It might be objected that virtue should be its own reward, but even if true, that could only apply to it when fully developed. Short of that, no one would be motivated to take the first steps toward it without this encouragement, which a belief in determinism would remove.

It would still be logically possible to teach determinism or fatalism, on the grounds that one's doing this is the effect of necessary causes. In this case, the belief that one could have an influence over others would be translated into a belief about efficient causality acting from one human agent to another. The results of this could be as self-confirming as those of a belief in free will, and this very fact shows that the world is not the inflexible thing which it would need to be for the determinist position. If we consistently act on the assumption that nothing depends on us, we will be sure to reach a situation where in fact nothing does: the external states follow the internal. But far from proving determinism, this example is simply a result of a perverse and self-destructive use of the will's creative potentiality. If the world itself were deterministic, all philosophies but one would fail the test of reality as soon as any attempt was made to apply them, whereas many self-consistent theories are workable to greater or lesser degrees.

Some consideration is given to the legal aspect of free will as well, as it can readily be shown that if necessity ruled everything, the law would be wrong in discriminating between cases where the offender acted voluntarily and where involuntarily. If in reality both kinds of action were equally necessary, the law would have to inflict the same penalty on both, or lack of penalty, as the case may be. Those who administered justice could maintain that they too were only acting under necessity, but this raises the psychological problem as to how one could remain active in the same way, while believing oneself to be under compulsion. However, the distinction between the voluntary and the involuntary in human affairs is carefully drawn by Aristotle in his *Nichomachean Ethics,* helped by the fact that the idea of this distinction is clear almost to the point of self-evidence, whereas determinism has nothing equally convincing on its side of the issue.

Alexander elsewhere[28] supplements the idea of man as a complex agent, with deliberation, choice, and decision, by a corresponding complexity in his motivation. This is defined in terms of the noble, the pleasurable, and the advantageous. These things seldom coincide, and the relation of the individual will to them is constantly changing. This means that one cannot expect the same man to act necessarily twice in the same way, even if the conditions were just the same, and his capacities were just the same. It only requires a slight readjustment of his relations to the three main classes of subjective motivation for him to behave quite differently, even where outwardly everything is the same.

This argument may serve to show a lack of necessity in human affairs, which is further strengthened by the fact that our memory of the last instance of a given act can just as easily make us repeat the action or choose another motive and act differently next time, but it does not fully vindicate free will. Free will cannot be equated with caprice and irregularity, even though it may give rise to them at times, because these things indicate changes in the will's direction, which in turn indicate a deficiency in one's perception of one's original objectives. Freedom is therefore best shown in a uniformity of action which is not caused from without, while having the capacity for changes when the same means do not suit the same ends.

28. *On Fate,* Mantissa, 174, 1–13.

Man is distinguished from the animals by the fact that he does not have to act in response to the mere appearances of things. He can also postpone his response while he enquires whether or not things really are as they appear. The Aristotelian origin of this argument can easily be seen in Book III of the *Ethics*, where things are classified according to whether they could or could not be subjects for deliberation. Among the things that are not subject to deliberation are things which happen predictably; also eternal truths; also things which are none of our business; and unpredictable and random events. What we do deliberate about are "things that are in our power and can be realized in action."

There is a difficulty here in that deliberation, according to Aristotle, seems to presuppose free will (it is that which is "in our power"), whereas Alexander uses deliberation itself as an argument for free will. The element of circularity here is best countered by the introduction of some third principle, the traditional argument that nature never causes anything in vain, or never implants a tendency in any creature with no object. If we can assume this, the mere fact that it is natural for us to deliberate would suffice to show that the options it weighs really exist, and that it governs the final decision.

What is Fate?

Although Alexander makes no more than a passing reference to astrology and prophecy, what he says is expressive of the soft determinism peculiar to them and to divination, where he explains that while all beings have a fate, they are not all necessarily ruled by it. His example in this regard is that of Zopyrus the physiognomist who said that Socrates must be a drunkard, according to his facial features. Socrates agreed that this would have been true as far as his own nature was concerned, but that by philosophical discipline he had become better than his nature, that is, better than his fate. This clearly reflects Alexander's idea, whereby fate would in every case be simply a native disposition or aptitude linked to persons or things which may govern them unless another is chosen.

Fate, therefore, is considered not to have even a conditional necessity. Even in relation to both inanimate things and living organisms, there is a "fate" which consists in the purpose for which they were made, and in the correct ways of using them. But this by no means guarantees that they will be put to their true purpose. The acorn which might give rise to another oak tree will probably be destroyed before it can germinate; where artifacts are concerned, no amount of understanding of their purpose can prevent their getting damaged or broken. Things can be put to uses which bear no relation to their natural purposes, as with wood, which is made into paper, utensils, furniture, although its natural purpose, and therefore its fate, in Alexander's terms, is to be the structural support of trees.

He proceeds to a definition of fate by reference to Aristotle's four causes, the formal, the material, the efficient, and the final. In this context, fate is regarded as essentially a form of efficient causality, being compared to the artist who makes a statue, only with the difference that it is held to be only one cause among others. It is also related to final causality, however, inasmuch as it brings about results which serve something else. A distinction is drawn between things which come into being for a purpose and those which do not, and "fated" things are assigned to the former. The latter, which includes trifling things such as fidgeting, are in the above sense uncaused inasmuch as they have no purpose or final cause. What is fated is confined to a subdivision of purposive events, those which happen by nature, and not those of them which result from reason.

It could be said that this philosophy concedes too much to popular thinking, which typically does not probe deeply enough to discover very many universal and necessary relations, such as would go well beyond the rather mild form of determination which he has in mind. He is right in drawing attention to the sector of the natural order in which a soft determinism is the case, only wrong in extending it everywhere. Also, it is interesting that a philosophy which attaches itself intentionally to a common sense point of view should introduce the conception of "real nothings" in nature, upon which the metaphysical heart of the subject depends. This does not weaken the argument, but the real aim is a reaction against the exaggerated claims made by the Stoics for necessity in all things. If the case for freedom is consequently exaggerated, that does not lessen the importance of the ideas involved.

4

The Three Grounds
of Freedom Compared

Plato's Freedom and Necessity

Among the comparisons to be made between Plato, Plotinus and
Alexander of Aphrodisias, some ideas of St.Augustine will be
included, as he was directly influenced by both Plato and Plotinus in
his own theory of free will. That there are interrelationships between
what the above philosophers thought about free will results from the
influence of Plato on the others, and the fact that Plato and Plotinus
both held a distinctive position on free will. Despite the paucity of
direct references to it in their writings, it was of central importance
to them.

It is therefore necessary to discuss an idea of free will which exists
only implicitly in Plato, and also largely so in Plotinus, but this can
be justified by the special nature of free will itself. It is so central an
issue that it is hardly possible for any developed philosophy not to
have at least an implicit position in regard to it. In all thought concerning the possession of moral virtue free will is inescapable.
Where Plato, Plotinus, and Augustine are concerned, it is thus possible to see an innate principle in regard to what constitutes freedom, and a corresponding depreciation of common sense views
about it. Alexander and Aristotle, however, approach free will from
the point of view of particular actions which it seems must be called
free, rather than from that of a theoretically innate freedom.

Plato's idea of free will can be seen in his conception of body
and soul, and the ways in which they are related. In this way, he
raises the issue of freedom and unfreedom in the center of the person himself, whereas the more monistic approach of Aristotelian

thought requires that it be found in relations between the individual and the outside world. A further contrast between Plato and Alexander lies in their ideas of chance and necessity. For the former, chance events are part of the realm of necessity, on the grounds that there could only be freedom in conjunction with intelligence and teleology. For Alexander, chance events are used in a more common sense manner to show that necessity does not rule everything.

Wherever Plato speaks of the cultivation of reason, he is referring implicitly to an actualization of a fuller degree of free will. Reason is held to be more ancient than the material world, and so belongs by definition outside the realm of necessity. But reason and necessity are not always mutually exclusive, since much in the world consists in a co-operation between them, this being the heading of the third part of the *Timaeus*, which is mainly concerned with the constitution of man. The possibility of any such co-operation implies that necessity comprises a good deal of discontinuous determinism as well as continuous, though this distinction is not drawn by Plato, probably because his negative evaluation of the material world in contrast with the forms did not encourage the discovery of general distinctions within it.

The sort of necessity which could co-operate with freedom would in fact have to be one in which the causal series were always short, being frequently broken and interrupted by others in a manner which would permit the entry of non-physical causes, that is, rational agents. This is the manner in which I have previously argued for a discontinuous determinism in the natural order, which would not exclude free will, but it should be noted at this point that there is no need for this conception of necessity to embrace the whole of nature. For the free will of noumenal causal agents to be able to exist in conjunction with the natural order, it is necessary only that a certain part of the natural order should function in a continuously necessary manner. To require that this causal order should extend everywhere would destroy the ideas of both freedom and necessity equally, as Plotinus argued.

Plato's examination of necessity did not extend much beyond what I refer to as discontinuous determinism, partly because the physical sciences were in their infancy in his time, and partly because his main concern was in any case with man, who is not normally subject to continuous determination within his experience. For this reason, he was able to include chance happenings within the kind of necessity he had in mind. Plotinus, on the other hand, is less concerned with nature than Plato is, whence his ideas about freedom are concentrated on the Platonic idea of the rational agent. Thus he is largely unaffected by questions as to how freedom can be possible amid so much that is not free. For him, soul is the indubitable reality which needs no proof, while he regarded the material world from the point of view of its incoherence and instability in comparison with its ideal-forms, more than it was so regarded by Plato. Thus Plotinus was even less interested in the world as a realm of necessary laws, except in connection with astronomy.

This modification of Plato's position is taken still farther by Augustine, and by much of Medieval thought with him. Plato himself acquired this tendency, partly from Socrates, who deliberately made man the center of his speculation, in reaction against the naturalist philosophers, and partly from his first teacher, Cratylus, who as an extreme Heraclitean, left him convinced of the evanescence of everything material, and of the need for another kind of reality in which eternal truths could be found.

This increasingly negative attitude to nature, which develops through Plato, Plotinus, and Augustine, is closely connected with what I would call the absolutist conception of freedom which developed among them at the same time.

From the start, the metaphysically inferior status of the natural world reflected inevitably upon actions performed in it, thus transferring the perception of value, and also of freedom, from the active to the contemplative life. Plato, however, is ambivalent in this regard, because in some places he teaches this attitude directly, while in others his involvement in legal and political matters seems to gainsay it.

Plato's idea of reason-as-freedom appears in the *Timaeus*, where the archetypal reason of the Demiurge is a causal agent "overruling" necessity in order to create a world. As man is said to be formed of body and soul in a manner analogous to the universe itself, the implication of this is that the use of our individual reason must likewise prevail over the instances of necessity that affect ourselves. If this were not so, there would be little meaning in the analogy between man and the cosmos which Plato works out so elaborately; a principle which can create a world, in its human instances, should be able to effect changes in it, once created. Thus although free will as such is not discussed by Plato, there need be no doubt about his belief in what is implicit in it.

Plotinian Freedom

We can also find the implicit idea of free will in Plotinus where he says that all actions contrary to wisdom are fated, since this absence of a direct reference to it is accompanied by a view of the fundamental options that we must choose between. Here he also shares Plato's idea that fate or necessity consists in a discontinuous determinism, at least to the extent that man is able to escape it. But in *Republic* X, 616, Plato explains by means of the myth that the cosmos ultimately rests on a continuous determinism, symbolized by the spindle of adamant upon which it turns. Here is the element of real necessity in the world, which Alexander is not willing to admit. Both kinds of necessity are thus parts of the world, and man's freedom lies in his ability to transcend its control, not so as to be capricious, but rather so as to realize a superior, more spiritual kind of necessity. This seems to be the main reason why Plato does not name free will explicitly, namely, its aspect of mere changeability, which was for him the hallmark of the inferiority of matter. An important passage in the *Epinomis* reveals his idea of freedom as a higher form of necessity:

> And of all necessitation, that which comes from a soul endowed with intelligence is far the mightiest, seeing she imposes her law as a sovereign who is subject to none, and when a soul has decided for the best with faultless wisdom, the utterly irreversible result falls out entirely to its mind. Adamant itself could be no stronger nor more inflexible, and 'tis no more than the truth to say that a triple Fate ensures and watches over the full accomplishment of all that each and every god has determined. . . . For mankind it should have been proof that the stars and their whole

procession have intelligence, that they act with unbroken uniformity, because their action carries out a plan resolved on from
countless ages; they do not change their purpose confusedly. . . .
Yet most of us have imagined the very opposite; because they act
with uniformity and regularity, we fancy them to have no souls.
Hence the mass has followed the leading of fools; it imagines that
man is intelligent and alive because he is so mutable, but deity,
because it keeps to the same orbits, is unintelligent.[1]

Neither Plato nor Plotinus distinguishes very clearly between the
freedom of actual possession of freedom, and the freedom to
choose between freedom and unfreedom, but in any case the very
possibility of such a progress to an immutable good has the effect of
casting doubt on any apparent free choice which might divert man's
energies in directions not consistent with it. In one passage, Plotinus actually speaks of the possession of the good as though it were
itself a kind of endless procession:

[The] Soul encompasses all, and so the cosmos moves, seeking
everything. Yet never to attain? On the contrary, this very motion
is its eternal attainment. Or, better; the Soul is ceaselessly leading
the Cosmos towards itself: the continuous attraction communi-
cates a continuous movement—not to some outside space but
towards the Soul and in the one sphere with it, not in the straight
line (which would ultimately bring the moving body outside and
below Soul), but in the curving course in which the moving
body at every stage possesses the Soul that is attracting it and
bestowing itself on it.[2]

These views on the circular pattern of the cosmic movement are
followed by a conception of the relation of the Soul to God which
would seem to be the archetype of the former:

The Soul exists in revolution around God to whom it clings in
love, holding itself to the utmost of its power near to Him as the

1. *Epinomis*, 982, b–d.
2. *Enn.* II, 2, 1.

The Three Grounds of Freedom Compared

Being on which all depends; and since it cannot coincide with God, it circles about Him.[3]

These closely-related passages show the idea of analogy between the relation of the physical world to the world-soul, and the soul to God, besides which they seem to echo the idea of the vision of the forms as a kind of procession, given in the *Phaedrus*. If possession comprises a kind of progression, so progression may be a virtual possession; freedom must therefore first involve a movement toward the good, and it attains its completeness when this movement is unchangeable. The same idea of freedom is forcefully expressed by Augustine in the *City of God,* where he concludes with his account of the heavenly Jerusalem:

Nor shall they not have free will, because sins shall not delight them. For it shall be more free being freed from the delight of sinning to an indeclinable and steadfast delight of not sinning. For the first free will, which was given to man, when he was created righteous, had power not to sin, but it also had power to sin: but this last free will shall be more powerful than that, because it shall not be able to sin.[4]

It should be noted how well this passage agrees with the Plotinian idea of free will, whereby the common sense idea of it would only be a semi-freedom. In the view of Plato, Plotinus, and Augustine, therefore, the function of choosing between courses of action is rather a sign of lack of freedom, which for them is only to be perfected by the absence of any possibility of change for the worse. Such is the idea of free will which may be called absolutist, and it contrasts with the modern empiricistic one which takes it for the potentiality of an unlimited range of options, with a significant concession to the quantitative aspect thereby. Part of the reason for this contrast lies in the dualistic conception of soul and body and of man and the world which was held by the ancients, and which has

3. Ibid., II, 2, 2.
4. *The City of God,* bk. XXII, chap. XXX.

been generally denied by the moderns. Among the ancient philosophers themselves, it is noteworthy that those who, like Aristotle and Alexander, saw the soul as more or less integral with the body and not a separable reality, were also inclined to the relative or pluralistic idea of free will.

The role of dualism in this connection is accentuated by the dual idea of the soul itself in Plato, and which is developed by Plotinus, for whom the fundamental choice is founded on the conception of a higher and a lower soul-phase.[5] In particular, this follows from Plato's idea of the creation, in the *Timaeus,* where the rational and irrational parts of the soul are produced separately. Natural forces are thought to act on and with the lower soul, but not on the rational as long as it is able to preserve its rationality, whence man's very constitution presents his will with a choice between what is logically prior to and what is posterior to the instancing of the forms.

In this connection, Plotinus speaks of "the essential of the Soul", and "that lower phase of the soul", in which affections and passions arise.[6] "For every human being is of a twofold character; there is that compromise-total (the lower soul or Couplement) and there is the Authentic Man: "To the remoter Soul, the pure, the sun and stars communicate no baseness.""[7] Here we have our intrinsic basis for free will, because neither of these two soul-phases has any *necessary* hegemony over the whole person; the will must choose.

The tendencies attributed to the two soul-phases also appear under the symbolism of the two horses and their driver in the chariot allegory in the *Phaedrus.* There, Plato is again concerned with an essential duality of choice for man:

Within each one of us there are two sorts of ruling or guiding principle that we follow: one is innate desire for pleasure, the other an acquired judgement that aims at what is best ... now one gains the mastery, now the other."[8]

---

5. Enn. IV, 3, 31.
6. Enn. II, 3, 9.
7. Ibid.
8. *Phaedrus* 237d–e.

These ruling tendencies are further referred to as "two kinds of madness, one resulting from human ailments, the other from a divine disturbance of our conventions of conduct."[9]

Before commenting on this conception, we should note how it compares with Alexander's conception of the internal complexity of man, which he analyzed under the two headings of his functions and his motives, namely the deliberation, the choice, the decision, and the whole man; and the noble, the pleasurable and the advantageous. Here the internal complexity is much more than simply dual, while also being rather accidental than substantial or ontological in man, though their interactions serve equally well in accounting for free will.

The Augustinian Perspective

In what was just quoted above, the higher passion was referred to as an "acquired judgement", contrary to what one might expect from the place given the rational soul by Plato. This is because in the natural life-history, the earliest contact with the outside world creates a condition in which the irrational prevails, and which can only be slowly reversed by education. The ontologically but not chronologically primary impulse toward reason and truth must thereby be restored to the central place in the personality by many efforts of will.

This dual property of the soul is also taken up by Augustine, inasmuch as it has a phase common to the whole soul of the animal, with another consisting in reason and knowledge:

> The human soul, however, because the instruments it uses, reason and knowledge—and it is with these we are concerned now—are far superior to the senses, makes itself independent, as far as it can, of the body, and gives first preference to the joy experienced within; and according as it turns aside to the senses, the greater the likeness it gives man to beast.[10]

9. *Phaedrus,* 265a.
10. *The Greatness of the Soul,* chap. 28, 54.

In the same book, the idea is developed that the consciousness of the senses is a function of a separate soul-phase. The lower is analyzed into the functions proper to vegetal, and then to animal life, maintaining the physical unity of the person by coordinating the various sensations. At what he calls the third level, he identifies what "belongs to man exclusively." This is analyzed into a series of internal divisions based on increasingly spiritual possibilities, whence the Augustinian treatment of the dual nature of the soul consists in a detailed working out of what is implicit in its higher and lower phases as taught by Plotinus.[11] In this respect, we can see a progressive development through Plato, Plotinus, and Augustine, and it is very significant for free will because of its elaboration of bases of activity which are consubstantial with us.

Because of his commitment to the doctrine that the impulse toward truth and real being is the one most essential to man, Plato is always obliged to say that man commits wrongs only against his own will, and likewise does not will to be deceived.[12] This same impulse is called the soul's "native vigor" by Augustine.[13] The soul is said to have an inherent kinship with abiding reality, though only the intelligence has direct access to it. This access is opposed by *epithymia*, the "many-headed" desiring principle, which is always turned toward the sensory world, and can draw the will away from the intellectual-principle. In this case, it is a false *eros*, and so essentially an alien accretion which obscures the real man. Plotinus' account of evil[14] is of just such a kind, and echoes Plato's version of this idea in the *Republic*, where the man with acquired evil is compared with the encrusted state of the sea-god Glaucus.

This helps explain the ascetic tendency in the moral teachings of Plato and Plotinus. If a preference for the intellectual faculty distances the personality from concern for sensuous or egotistic desires, as it evidently does, it would seem only natural to think that the causality in this connection could be reversed, with the

11. Ibid., chap. 33.
12. *Republic*, 413a.
13. *Therapeia*, chap. III, 4.
14. *Enn.* I, 8, 14.

expectation that an initial denial of the pleasure-seeking drives will result in a corresponding enlightenment of the intellect. The logic here is faulty, because a causality like the above is only necessary-but-not-sufficient, and is not reversible, unlike a hard causality. This has been often overlooked in the tradition which followed these philosophers, and they cannot be blamed for failures to put the world to rights which do not truly reflect their principles.

The distinction between the higher and lower soul-phases was discussed in the writings of the Fathers of the Church, who admitted the Platonic conception in the form of the distinction of *Animus* and *Anima*. This has been re-examined in modern times by C.G. Jung:

> In living men, the two correspond in a certain degree to the cerebral and sympathetic nervous system.... The *animus* is bright and active, the *anima* is dark and earth-bound.[15]

Each of these psychic realities has a very different meaning for free will. It is the peculiarity of the higher, or rational soul that it is not intrinsically bound to any specific function outside itself. Bound only by its rationality, it can play an active role in absolutely anything, in contrast with the lower or irrational soul, which is never able to work apart from the basic life processes which it exists to regulate. On these grounds alone, the supposedly free choice between these two realms of psychic life must also be a choice between two radically different kinds of freedom, or of choice. This again highlights the possibility of "choosing a choice", which has been referred to before, with its conception of quite different levels on which choices can be made.

The choice-of-choice extends also to ignorance and knowledge, as Plato shows in *Laws* 732a, where he refers to the difference between simply holding a wrong belief and having a passional attachment to it. This is the basis of what he calls "double" as opposed to simple ignorance. Here, false belief is adopted by the desiring or epithymetic principle, in which the action of the higher soul or *animus* is co-opted into the service of the lower, because it is

---

15. *The Secret of the Golden Flower*, Wilhelm, tr., introduction.

part of man's interior freedom of choice that his choice in favor of the relatively unfree principle should also involve the entrapment of the intrinsically free one for purposes it could not initiate for itself.

"Ascending" and "Descending" Volition

This entrapment would result in an outlook which was inverted in respect to that in which the rational soul was master, but nevertheless it is just as able to be self-confirming as the former, seemingly vindicating the passional choice. The fact that such contrary developments can be pursued without any obvious collision with reality is the basis of Plato's idea of folly. The cure for this is given in his moral teachings, where they center on a *katharsis* of the soul, used as a kind of therapy. This means not just the assimilation of information, or even ideas, but the habituation of the mind to principial norms which eventually leaven the will of the whole person.

No mention is made of the fact that such contrary options must have an important bearing on free will, if reality is flexible enough to be livable on either set of priorities. This duality of options results from the soul's ability to know the forms by their "descent" in the material world, or else by an "ascent" to their absolute nature, which is independent of sense-perception. The ontological ascent and descent are equally parts of the whole system of reality, and so must always coexist. Without this background, the moral conflict between good and evil would have little or no meaning. If no one could defy the norms of the ascending eidetic process without immediate danger, one would avoid doing so as one would avoid an oncoming train.

These two possibilities result from the fact that the instancing of the forms in matter is not bound to include the archetypal relations between them. All persons choose the realities they most want to fill their lives and thus complete their representations of the world, whether they are valid images of the original or not. In this way, one can be said to "create one's own reality." The "ascending" option means a selection of realities according to values, whereas the "descending" selects its realities according to purposes and criteria which have little or no significance in the whole of things.

The Three Grounds of Freedom Compared

Both ascending and descending systems of action are equally motivated by the Form of the Good, but this is because of the outgoing and returning movements equally, away from and towards the Good. However, the attraction of the Good has radically different meanings, depending on how the agent relates to the direction of instantiation. Thus, subjectively speaking, there may be very little difference between the attraction of the Good as perceived in itself and as reflected as it were, in instanced things with which it is falsely identified. The objective and essential difference, however, is total.

This accounts for another aspect of the distinction between good and evil, namely that no one does evil because it is evil, but only for the sake of what, taken by itself, is good, whereas to do good simply because it is seen to be good is both normal and rational. Where Plato says that no one willingly does wrong, it could well be this difference between good and evil which he has in mind. It would be quite right to say that the wrongdoer acts against his own will if the will is conceived as being specifically designed to be oriented toward the good, an idea which is at least supported by appearances. Even if somebody claims to be able to will evil because it is evil, he cannot expect to escape the implication that for him this course appears to have more of the good in it than any alternative.

Where Plotinus treats this aspect of good and evil, he makes use of the myth of Narcissus, making the water-borne reflection the equivalent of the physical form of the person, and the falling in love with the image results from a state of confusion between the archetypal realities and their appearance in matter, which is cunningly counterfeit, insubstantial, and utterly unstable. Evil for Plotinus is equally a mistaken aim at the Good and understood as a kind of alien accretion upon the soul. He can be seen to express the view of evil common to Socrates and Plato in the following:

> No: men are no doubt involuntary sinners in the sense that they do not actually desire to sin; but this does not alter the fact that wrong-doers, of their own choice, are, themselves, the agents . . . *if they were not agents they could not sin.*[16]

16. *Enn.* III, 2, 10 (my emphasis).

Here we also see evil associated with the minimal component of freedom, causal agency.

The connection between the above ideas and those of Alexander on free will is to be found in Plato's teachings in the *Laws*, which were in the first place an influence on Aristotle. In the *Laws*, Plato shows that his ideas on the subject of freedom are by no means confined to the absolutist position defined by the Good, which divides all human actions into three groups, those conducive to it, those indifferent to it, and those inimical to it. In this case, the latter classes of action could not be called free except in the doubtful sense that a road can give one the freedom to turn off onto other routes which will cause one to lose one's way. But in Book IX of the *Laws*, Plato shows that he also accepts the relative idea of freedom, without trying to prove any logical connection between it and the metaphysical idea.

Before turning to the more legally-orientated ideas of free will, it would be worthwhile at this stage to sum up the various meanings which are included under the conception of free will.

1) Transcendental freedom, with value alone as its criterion, in which one is outside the pressures of more relative choices.

2) Dynamical freedom, the ability to pursue a maximum number of objectives, regardless of their degrees of value.

3) Legal freedom, the freedom to act in ways which will not bring one into conflict with laws created for the preservation of society.

4) Moral freedom, the freedom to act in ways which are consistent with the truth as to what is best, where this is relevant to society in general.

5) Vocational or artistic freedom, that is, the freedom to pursue activities of a special nature within the bounds of a given set of technical principles.

Each of these conceptions has its own criteria of possibility and impossibility. The first could only be made impossible by its being confused with a form of practical activity whereas the only impossibility for the second would be the physically impossible. In the third and fourth, it is defined by the presence or absence of the values in question. In the fifth, the impossible lies in what conflicts with the nature of the work in question. Some combinations among these freedoms are possible, as where the fifth combines in different ways with each of the first four, but the deepest dividing-line is between the first, i.e., the transcendental, and the remaining four, the latter being wholly immanent freedoms in themselves.

Legal Functions of Free Will

The relation between Alexander's ideas of free will and Plato's comes by way of Aristotle, who was mainly influenced on this subject by Plato's *Laws*. In the latter, the idea of free will is wholly practical and dynamic, and it is even referred to by name, which strongly supports the idea that Plato always took it for granted in the rest of his writings. Book IX of the *Laws* is concerned with punishments, and so contains much that has a bearing on free will, while in *Laws* X 904c–d, free will is referred to directly.

To begin with, Plato discusses the problem of those who commit crimes as a result of some passion which they cannot control. Their guilt is a reality even if their desires are too strong for them, because he contends that they nearly always have other options by which they could change their course of action in a way which must presuppose free will. Further, he draws a clear distinction between voluntary and involuntary wrong in his own terms, which requires him to use a different word for wrong. He admits the universality of the distinction made by the law here, but maintains his principle that even the most deliberate offence is always against the will of the offender. As no one can be thought to forfeit the good willingly, the whole class of voluntary wrongs is for him therefore "involuntary", and so he has to use a word other than "wrongs" for those which are normally called involuntary wrongs. Citizens indirectly suffer "damage" from one another, both voluntarily and involuntarily, and this, it is said, should not be classed as a wrong at all.[17]

17. *Laws,* IX 861b–862c.

Here, Plato is trying to subject a legal question to his metaphysics. The reasoning is not satisfactory, because there is no hope that the involved parties would accept his distinction between "wrong" and "damage" when their interests are affected, but the implicit commitment to free will is clear enough. So it is also where he speaks of the infliction of wounds, where, as with murder, they are to be divided between those inflicted in passion, or in fear, or intentional and deliberate. (His avoidance of the voluntary aspect of wrong does not appear practicable here.) The public good suffers most from man's natural pursuit of the pleasurable and avoidance of the painful. The result of that for the individual is said to be one of self-caused blindness—very significant for free will—along with ignorance, and conceit of one's own wisdom,[18] and this brings ruin on the state. Full knowledge of this fact should be the remedy, but knowledge is very rare, as it involves much more than the holding of pieces of information, which can support only opinion.

In cases of attempted murder, the one who made the failed attempt is to be put on trial, but leniency is to be shown out of respect for the "tutelary power"[19] which has preserved the life of the one, and saved the other from incurring the curse of guilt. If the wrong-doer were treated exactly as if he *had* committed the intended crime, it would be tantamount to treating divine providence as nonexistent, which for Plato would be sacrilegious.

Man is also said to be either a master of his passions and pleasures or a slave to them, though he has no such mastery in regard to his ignorance[20] and knowledge, so that his moral limitations must be under his control in ways that his intellectual limitations are not. Wrong is always the result of man's being ruled by "passion, fear, pleasure, pain, envy, or cupidity," whereas right action results simply from its being performed in the belief that it is for the best. The primacy of intentions in this respect is emphasized here, where it is affirmed that such actions are still right, even if their results turn out to be harmful. As the passions in a ruling position are exclusively the

18. Ibid., 863c–d.
19. Ibid., 876e–877b.
20. Ibid., 863d.

sources of wrong, it follows that even false opinion can be the basis of right action, provided only that it be dispassionate.

Where the ultimate cause of moral evils is concerned, free will is referred to as such, "No man who believes in the gods as the law would have him believe has ever yet of his own free will done unhallowed deed or let slip lawless discourse."[21] There is an inconsistent (for Plato) implication here that wrongs are freely-willed, but Plato's own belief in free will is further emphasized by his contention that "persuasion" must be the means of converting the wrong-doer, who must above all else be persuaded of the existence of the Gods.

The importance of intentions is also shown by the fact that all killings committed in self-defense, whether among freemen or among slaves, shall not be counted as offences at all, though we are not told whether there has to be a trial to establish that self-defense was the motive. A curious mitigating circumstance in connection with murder is that if the victim forgives the killer before he dies,[22] the penalty is to be commuted to one year's banishment for ritual purity. This is comparable to the way in which the law must also bow to the "tutelary power" in connection with attempted crime. The choices of outside wills are therefore to be reckoned with, along with those of the judges, according to Plato, which further supports the voluntaristic principle.

Such is the conception of personal responsibility, and therefore of free will, which influenced Aristotle in his *Ethics,* which in turn influenced Alexander. He readily took up the idea of personal responsibility, and developed the logical grounds for it, commenting on Aristotle's *Topics* as follows:

> That if the opposite of what depends on us does not depend on us, not even what depends on us, itself, will depend on us.[23]

The idea of responsibility is accepted, but, beyond that, an objective criterion for its applicability is laid down; if something is really to depend on us, it must do so in both positive and negative senses.

---

21. *Laws* x, 885b.
22. *Laws* ix, 876e–877a and 869d–e.
23. *On Fate,* Quaestio ii, 4.

Thus if speaking depends on us, so also must our keeping silent, and as we can easily accept both these alternatives, our responsibility in this regard is settled. But at any given time, we are not able not to have the power of speech, whence it can be said that we are not responsible for our possession of it, either.

Deliberation and Assent

That something or other depends on us is said to be part of our nature, so it follows that it does not depend on us that something should depend on us. From the point of view of free will, this can be expressed such that we do not have the free will either to choose to have free will or not to have it. As it is a part of our nature, our freedom is therefore *necessary,* and with it our responsibility; such would seem to be the conclusion, though Alexander does not express it in quite this manner. His idea of it is "that something depends on us is in accordance with fate."[24] It is assumed to be impossible that nothing should depend on us.

That of which the opposite is impossible is defined as the *necessary,* but not as the fated, because the definition of fate used here is such that some kinds of necessity, like two and two making four, are not a matter of fate, because for Alexander fate comprises much that is not strictly necessary, there including all things which result from physical processes. This idea of fate makes it equivalent to "according to nature." However, one would not be any less free on account of one's freedom having resulted from a necessary cause, and in this case the necessity does not seem to be absolute.

Further on,[25] he closely follows what Aristotle says about deliberation,[26] where his equivalent of Aristotle's "voluntariness" is "assent". This is a means of proving that something does depend on us, and of defining the difference between human and animal behavior. The animals too have the power of assent, we are told, just as Aristotle agrees that they share in voluntariness, but in them it is

24. Ibid., Quaestio II, 5.
25. Ibid., Quaestio III, 13.
26. *Nichomachean Ethics*, bk. III, 1–5.

always linked more or less mechanically to sensory stimuli, such that they have no freedom to disengage from them or distance themselves from them in any way.

But man has deliberation (to which Aristotle adds Choice), in addition to assent, which means that his assent need never be automatic, but rather that he can rationally consider the object to decide whether it actually is what it seemed to be at first sight. His assent is given or withheld accordingly. Thus when we say that something depends on man, we mean that something depends on his power of deliberation. If, then, deliberation, as an ability not to assent to mere appearances, belongs to us beyond doubt, it will be right to make the above assumption that it is impossible that nothing should depend on us.

Alexander notes the fact that, according to the above reasoning, this last conclusion would not follow if man invariably deliberated on his impressions, because in that case he would not be able not to do so, whence it would not depend on him, in accordance with what was said before about both the positive and negative powers being jointly necessary. Instead, his deliberation would be merely one more part in a sequence of events which would be just as necessary as the behavior norms of animals, only being a few degrees more complex. But this possibility does not arise because we do in fact very commonly assent to appearances without deliberating. But even where we neglect to deliberate, there is always an element of freedom in our assent, because the ways in which we give assent vary, depending on circumstances.

This fact, that we sometimes act with both deliberation and assent, and sometimes with assent alone, is vital for our judgement of guilt in the light of free will, as Plato again makes clear in *Laws* IX,[27] where he calls for specially severe penalties for crimes committed "in downright wickedness, and of deliberate design." Alexander also instances for a different purpose the fact that there is always praise for those who act with due deliberation, and blame for those who do not, because, assuming that this is rational behavior, it shows that we know that deliberation does depend on us, in

27. *Laws*, 869a–e.

which case it must be part of our causal power. It is clear that he understands this in the Kantian manner of man being free to initiate a new causal series, for in the same connection he says:

> For having these things depending on himself is the same as being a beginning and an efficient cause of those things which we say depend on himself."[28]

Further on, he again describes man as a "beginning" as well as the cause of the things done by him. Alexander's treatment of free will can thus be seen to be a direct development of the legal conception of it in Plato's *Laws*, following closely upon Aristotle's. His identification with Aristotle's thought is such that even when he considers the metaphysical aspect of free will, he ignores Plato's thought in that connection, and uses only Aristotle's metaphysics of Privation. The difference between him and Plotinus on this subject, and in many other ways, is substantial, but both can nevertheless be shown to derive from Plato's thought, such was its great and unsystematic width.

In terms of the five concepts of freedom listed above, the main divergence between Plotinus and Alexander is owing to Plotinus' concentration on the first, the transcendental, and Alexander's concentration on the second, third, and fourth, the immanent concepts. The fifth is ambivalent, because it can either be an extension of the latter, or it can form part of the first. But despite the distinctions involved here, the expression "free will" is still used in connection with them all, which indicates that there is some more general conception involved in all of them.

The Necessity of Freedom

I shall next consider the argument that no freely-willed action can be self-destructive, such that freedom could destroy the use of freedom itself. A supposed freedom to become unfree is a dubious conception because such an option lies on the plane of action which, by the criterion in Chapter 2 implies that even the freedom it starts

---

28. *On Fate*, Mantissa, XXIII, 173, 1.

from is only a semi-freedom. As shown in the same chapter, actions in that category, pursued in defiance of the normative patterns or ideal forms, tend to reduce freedom to nothing and so involve an essential self-contradiction, though that does not make them impossible.

Consequently, the fully free action must be such as to conserve the being of the agent, and that of his world, as he depends on the latter. There are innumerable different degrees to which being can be conserved and strengthened, and the soundness of being is most clearly measured in terms of unity and harmony. This means that the most minimally free action must be at least practically beneficial, while the most free will be creative. Scientifically speaking, such actions will thus amount to local reductions in entropy, and therefore be reversals of the general cosmic movement, which is always towards maximum probability, and therefore to disorder and disunity.

The good and real being are inseparable, whence there is an interconnection between freedom, unity, being, and good, all of which admit of very different degrees. But what of the case of the partially free action which enhances the being of the agent, but does just the opposite for other persons and things in the world around him? Here, one can only draw a balance between the good he does himself with the harm he does to others. If the latter is slight in relation to the former, his action may still be free according to the full criteria, but if it becomes a question of the good of one being directly at the expense of that of others, it will not be.

The free action conserves or enhances the being of the agent and his world, because the two are inseparable. A good realized at the expense of others is a breach of unity, and therefore of being and good. The selfish calculation is therefore a miscalculation because the being of all concerned depends on unity, which this miscalculation disrupts. These considerations apply most directly to affairs on the material plane, the unequal sharing of material goods in cases where all have equal rights to them; a strictly spiritual selfishness would be by no means so easy to define because it is hard to specify what may have been taken from others.

On the other hand, mere differences between persons are not in themselves examples of disunity, despite appearances. Whatever fosters the development of one individual becomes the same as what fosters the development of the world, inasmuch as he is a part of it, and it is through the individual that the higher possibilities are realized. Conversely, when individuals are artificially restricted to one single level, the likelihood of conflict and competition for the same things is greatest.

What has been said from the point of view of unity and being can also be said from that of possibility and impossibility. When we say that the free action fosters the being of the agent and his world, we mean thereby that it is aimed at a true possibility, one which is not self-contradictory. All action aimed at the impossible results in disunity and dissipation of being, because it consists essentially in a destructive collision between some form of energy and some object which is not amenable to it; what by nature should have produced new order has been misdirected so as to produce the exact opposite. This implicitly involves a greater or lesser cancellation of the agent's power to act, whence neither can it be freely-willed according to the above premise that the freely-willed action enhances the being of the agent.

But the freedom to annul freedom does involve some act, and therefore some residuum of freedom, such as has already been considered in regard to causal agency without knowledge. With free will connected to unity and being, and thence to possibility, we can now see how possibility enters into all five of the criteria named above. It overcomes the dividing-line between the first and the four relative ones, because the freedoms contained in the latter can all be practically beneficial and creative in diverse ways, while the first necessarily is so, in a more simple and direct way.

Of all the categories of free will, only the first involves pure possibility, because insofar as it is true to its principle, there is no practical impossibility it could encounter, as it transcends by definition the order of relative conditions which impede and exclude one another. In regard to the four immanent freedoms, each is liable to meet with impossibilities in its own way. This gives us a further reason for distinguishing the latter from the first, closely related to their dependence on occasional causes, as has been observed before in regard to Plotinus.

The Three Grounds of Freedom Compared

Relative freedoms have the effect of enlarging the total of possibilities for freedom, in addition to the absolute freedom, rather as the numbers less than ten realize separately the numerical possibilities implicit in this number. The idea of possibility being the interrelating factor in regard to all forms of free will differs only aspectually from that of knowledge, because the choice of the truly possible and the avoidance of the impossible clearly depends on knowledge. This conclusion fits well with the Socratic idea that wrong-doing is only a form of ignorance, since we are bound to be more likely to will the impossible the more ignorant we are.

An example of ignorant, and therefore unfree will in action would arise in every case where an effect was desired, though without regard to the natural means whereby it could be brought about. This would apply to all attempts to get something for nothing, ranging from the making of supposed perpetual-motion machines to theft or forgery. The question as to whether one can will the impossible while still being the cause of one's action is complicated by the fact that the nature of the human cause changes with the passage of time, so there would be one answer at the start of the activity, and another at the end. In regard to the latter, a cause which was *de jure* the cause of its own ceasing to exist (the ultimate effect of willing the impossible), should not even be able to begin to exist. Therefore, as it has begun to exist, it must first have been directed to something other than self-destruction, and then changed to an unfree ruling passion. The minimal initial freedom is thus dissipated in this change, since willing the impossible cannot be free, except in the minimal causal sense.

At this stage, it is appropriate to make a transition from arguments for free will to arguments more particularly related to its natural consequence, moral responsibility. But in the light of the form of thought employed in the previous chapters, there is a significant difference made to the meaning of this transition. Ordinarily understood, it follows that the more absolutely free will is established, the more absolute the resulting moral responsibility will be.

However, in the present case free will has been treated in a metaphysical manner which takes us beyond common sense ideas of it, in that it is only fully actual if there is a positive tendency of the will toward values, and away from engagement in relativities for their own sake. It must be noted that this condition is incompatible with situations and states of mind in which one is liable to commit moral offences. Absolute freedom of the will is defined as a freedom in and for the good and the true. St.Augustine was quoted in this connection to show that this is a part of Platonism which he took over for Christianity not only unchanged, but even accentuated, and this should help confirm the universality of the conception.

Its consequence for moral responsibility, however, is that when one does wrong one has already departed from the fullest degree of free will, and this means that moral responsibility can never be absolute, no matter how certainly that responsibility is established. Conversely, there appears the paradox that absolute guilt can only be incurred by those with absolute free will who, in the light of the foregoing, are those who do not do any wrong and have no disposition to do so.

This conclusion alone would be misleading, however. On the one hand, it is a theoretical reason for tempering justice with mercy and for the Christian belief in forgiveness for sins which are repented of; but on the other it appears to make absolute guilt impossible. If that were so, man would be beneath the level of spirit, and free will would have no meaning. In reality, behavior which is only relatively guilty can develop into absolute guilt, despite the lack of full knowledge. If the behavior is deliberately repeated for long enough, it amounts to an assertion of full knowledge, and that suffices to make it morally equivalent to actions done with real knowledge. This is an abuse of free will to the point at which it is lost, and involves a subjective form of certainty about something wholly untrue. This deception is willed, and that can only mean the self-destructive case of willing the impossible, and this possibility underlies the importance of the issues of moral responsibility in what follows.

5

Moral Responsibility: For and Against

Questions of Practical Importance

The being who is metaphysically free is thereby in some real way the author of his own actions, and so is said to be morally responsible. I shall add more to what has been said to establish the reality of this condition, in a way which will not be affected by the prevailing social beliefs about it. No matter how much or how little anecdotal evidence there may be for it, the arguments will not be affected, since they relate to what man essentially is, and not to what he may happen to be, and because of the paradox of freedom itself, that freedom cannot impose any necessity on its possessor to develop it.

Two clearly contrasting positions will be compared, and their ideas will be applied to the present subject. Hume has made particularly penetrating criticisms of the ideas involved in moral responsibility, for which reason counter arguments to them will have to be found. My treatment of Hume may need some explanation, because I am using some of his arguments so as to construct some strong possible objections to moral responsibility, and not so as to provide a balanced account of his thought. It may involve exaggerating some of the negative implications of his arguments, so as to bring out the issue involved more clearly, and presenting them in a more systematic manner than may have been intended, for the same reason.

The practical denial of moral responsibility may not run into immediate difficulties because of the self-fulfilling principle which enters into human beliefs, which allows scope for all but the most irrational behavior to some degree. Thus the increasing organization of society, with its regulation of nearly all activities, inevitably has the effect of lessening the need for moral responsibility, and therefore the incentive to achieve it. This points to the possibility of a future world which would be so completely organized that the idea of moral responsibility might become as redundant as the skills of hunters in pre-modern times. A society where every activity was regulated by a separate force of officials, backed by electronic surveillance, is not only theoretically possible, but is already some way to being realized.

One objection to such a development would be that it would annul the need for much that results from the normal development from childhood to adulthood, such that human beings could remain in many respects children all their lives. This would be specially objectionable if human life had a purpose beyond those invented for it by society. This purpose could in fact be understood as the overcoming of what C.G. Jung called *participation mystique,* the ignorant confusion of the self with what is alien to it. If this is part of the purpose of life, the stifling or denial of moral responsibility would frustrate life's deepest purpose.

Another objection would be that a society without moral responsibility would be very unstable, because nearly all of its ability to function would be concentrated in a single artificial and probably vulnerable system, instead of being distributed among innumerable individuals. It would differ from a morally responsible society in much the same way as a machine differs from an organism. Whereas living organisms can survive a great deal of damage because their parts are partially self-subsistent, a machine need only fail in one part to fail as a whole.

These considerations, ranging from the metaphysical to social practicality are in fact closely involved with the results of maturation from childhood. Man has an innate knowledge of what he really is, which makes him irreconcilable with being permanently a child, or drunk, or permanently in any other irresponsible condition.[1] This is a matter of the acquisition, or the failure to acquire, a range of possibilities based on free will.

The possibilities of developing free will and moral responsibility

1. Aristotle, *Protrepticus,* 96.

can even be assimilated to the possibilities of living a life of physical health or one of sickness. The instinctive choice of health is not affected by considerations that there may be a world with ideal medical care, in which one could be permanently ill with safety and dignity, analogously to the universal surveillance which could theoretically replace moral responsibility. What is involved here affects us almost as critically as the choice of life or death, to which it is in any case related. Although the normal instinctive reactions exist whether responsibility is real or not, it makes a significant difference whether we accept moral responsibility in the belief that it is purely and simply a form of instinctive behavior, or whether we do so with the idea that it is logically well founded. This is the more difficult option for which argument is needed.

Some Opposing Arguments

Hume's point of departure is the wholly determined nature of physical causes and effects. The "actions of matter" are taken to be always necessary. At the same time, he has his own distinctive way of regarding cause and effect. He denies that we ever know what causal power itself is; we just get used to seeing things happen in certain sequences. That these sequences never vary is what for him constitutes causal necessity. Union between the phenomena and our inference from this experienced conjunction is all-essential here. Similarly, he holds that there is just the same union between the different states of the mind as there is between physical forces, since he follows the Berkeleyan assimilation of objects to series of "ideas",[2] although he accepts the Newtonian conception of their laws.

Necessity is said to arise from "constant union alone", although we are thought to have no insight into the actual mechanisms of physical necessity. This lack of insight is not thought to detract from the necessity, though, and this is a point worth comparing with the assertion that we can know the instantiation of the forms, despite not knowing the actual mechanism of that, either.

On this basis, our actions are said to have an equally constant

2. *Treatise*, bk. II, part III, sec. 1.

union with our motives and tempers and circumstances. Hume gives a number of pairs of examples illustrating necessity in the relations between material things and human motives and actions. The uniformity of human actions is held to be just as great as that of material things. Such comparisons have a *prima facie* validity, but they do not throw any light on the question of our being able to choose among the motives which prompt the different kinds of action. Disproof of free will calls for more than a necessary connection between motive and action; one must also prove an inability to choose alternatives among the motives. Hume tends to conflate the will with natural causality, so as to reconcile them, but this widens the definition of causality too much for it to be effectual. Also, his analysis uses the backwards-looking perspective on events, from which they always appear more determined than from the temporally forwards-looking one. But real life is lived just as much before and during events as after them.

The validity of moral evidence is instanced in opposition to our usual ideas of free will, the fact that people act in accordance with their characters, and can normally be relied upon to do so. Thus for Hume, there would be no difference, in regard to freedom and necessity, between a prince presuming on the obedience of his subjects, and a sailor presuming on the wind's power to move his ship. The will would be just one more natural cause. At the same time, however, he excludes caprice from any title to freedom, (an unusual agreement with Plato), since the most extreme form of capriciousness would be madness, in which no one ever sees any freedom. But if freedom is not to be found in erratic or capricious behavior, Hume could still be claiming too much in also excluding it from the contrary cases where the will works predictably. Freedom comes from a transition from a lower set of laws to a higher, not from an abandonment of law as such.[3]

It would have been more consistent for Hume to have equated the "system of liberty" with mere caprice and randomness. In this way, the attack on free will would have had a much more specific target, instead of being deployed ubiquitously, as though the idea of

---

3. See Chapter 4, quotation from *Epinomis*.

free will had arisen from nothing at all. However, liberty of indifference, though it is a part of free will, is not necessary for moral responsibility, as it is the actual causality of the will which is decisive in that regard.

Another example we are given is that of a prisoner, to whom the will of the jailer is a more implacable obstacle than the very walls and bars of the prison. It is essential to Hume's argument that "the system of liberty" should imply the negation of causal necessity, and if we admit the existence of a series of necessary causes and effects, and that from any given cause only one effect can follow, freedom will duly be ruled out. But we are not given sufficient grounds for the second of these two admissions. There is a hiatus between the assertion that some necessary cause must operate, and the assertion that only one can operate at a given time; there is nothing to exclude the possibility that there are many potential causes for every actual effect. Where a cause is artificially isolated, as in the laboratory, something like the Humian necessity will prevail, but that only underlines its lack of applicability to the world in general.

Where there are many causal agencies in operation, there is no knowing which causal series will intersect with which. Thus a ship which keeps out water under normal conditions may not do so in very rough weather, but in either case, that of a successful voyage, or the sinking of the ship, everything will proceed according to a series of strict causal necessity. Natural causal agencies constantly supervene upon one another, whence there is nothing preternatural in the idea of the human will exerting some such role. Hume himself acknowledges this,[4] where he admits that different causes can render one another's operation uncertain.

That Hume's assimilation of the human will to the forces of natural causality depends on an inadequate idea of causality is to be seen from what has been observed by other philosophers in connection with examples where a human being can be made to act in ways no different from that of a material object. If one trips and falls full length, what is involved does not differ from the falling over of a piece of timber of the same size and weight as oneself. As human

4. *An Enquiry Concerning Human Understanding*, sec. VIII, pt. I, p. 89.

beings comprise material elements, all drawn from the non-living world, it is only logical that, to the extent that they are so composed, they should be subject to the laws which govern matter everywhere. Failing this, chemical matter would have to lose its essential nature upon becoming part of a living being, whereas no such change is ever observed. Just as it would be irrational to expect matter to cease to be itself in a living organism, so it would be equally irrational to expect that, after the addition of life, the matter in question should still be governed exclusively by its own laws. The truth here is a *via media* between the extremes of a transformation of matter by life, and of an effective reduction of life to the matter to which it was added. The composite being will therefore be ruled by two sets of laws at the same time, though continually changing in their relative proportions.

Three Natures in Man

If, however, intelligence or rational will is added to the combination of matter and life, it would be reasonable to expect that this composite being would be governed by three sets of laws. This can be illustrated by the knee-jerk reflex. This upward movement of the leg belongs within the laws which apply to us insofar as we are living organisms. Alternatively, we might just decide to move the leg, and raise it in just the same way voluntarily, in which case it is the laws of the rational agent that apply. Finally, some outside force could act upon the leg to raise it a little, as though it were a piece of wood attached to something by a hinge. In this third case, the action belongs to us according as we are mere assemblies of matter, whose laws apply in this case.

Similarly, there are three ways in which we may be fed: we may eat because it is the set time to do so (rational agent); because hunger makes us do so (living organism); or because we are being force-fed, (material object). Clearly three kinds of causality operate in us in these things, but Hume's idea of causality is too vague to comprehend them, since it does not go beyond mere succession, as though breakfast was the cause of dinner, or day of night. If such a vague conception of causality can in some sense embrace both human wills and natural causes, it need not involve any very deep understanding of it, therefore.

No one could imagine that because a human being falling off a cliff descends with an acceleration of thirty-two feet per second per second—just like a stone—he therefore could not also be the kind of being with the capacity to eat and reproduce. Likewise, his material and organic natures cannot be thought to exclude yet higher orders of possibility. In reality we are at once rational agent, living organism, and material object, and subject to the laws of all three without any mutual interference. For this reason it is useless to argue against the free will proper to the rational agent by adding to our knowledge of the ways in which we are subject to the laws of the other two. What science discovers about our role as living organisms and material bodies could be increased to infinity without detracting anything from the activity proper to the rational agent.

Determinism requires that the causation of human actions be no different from that which applies to everything in the non-living world. This can be made to sound reasonable, until we see its necessary presupposition, namely, that life and intelligence are in themselves nothing, causally speaking, in relation to the interactions of matter. But being, life, and intelligence have long been recognized as the three most universal and irreducible principles, as in Proclus' *Elements of Theology*,[5] which is the metaphysical background to the natural conviction that life and intelligence are both causal principles in their own right. There is a relative sense in which life and mind *are* null in relation to matter, which lies simply in their not being material, but this differs completely from the causal nullity required by determinism.

This brings us to the question as to how such different things can be supposed to interact. The difficulty involved in this is made to seem greater because we naturally tend to overrate our understanding of the interactions between things of the same nature, simply because we constantly observe them happening. But in fact there is no way in which logic can show us that a billiard ball must be made

5. *El. Theol.,* props. 101, 102, 103.

to move when struck by one which is moving. That motion is communicable from one material thing to another is just a brute fact with which we feel at home, not a theorem, since the laws of mechanics only follow experience, and do not prescribe it. Thus the mere difficulty of conceiving any kind of interaction is not necessarily an argument against it, just as, for Hume, our inability to know the inner workings of causal connections does not detract from our knowledge of their necessity. Here again, the panacea of constant conjunction would seem to answer everything and nothing.

Hume also asserts that there is no such thing as liberty of indifference, because the lack of any sense of constraint on our will is not enough to prove that our will is not in point of fact determined. The subjective feeling of freedom is nevertheless accompanied by a causal connection between the motives and the action which remains the same even in cases where compulsion is known to be involved. Human actions would be as predictable as those of natural forces, he maintains, if the observer was "perfectly acquainted with every circumstance of our situation and temper, and the most secret springs of our complexion and disposition."[6]

There is an assumption here, to the effect that what is comprised in "the most secret springs" will be of the same nature as what is comprised in the natural phenomena they relate to. But this inner reality is just as likely to be secret (that is, non-empirical), by its very nature, as it is to be so just because it has not yet been found. In Kantian terms, Hume is speaking of the inner source of motivation as though he knew it was one more phenomenon. If he was right in that respect, his argument would otherwise be sound, but there is no compelling reason to allow that the will-principle is phenomenon and not noumenon, because the subject's inability to perceive himself need not be taken to be the same as non-existence, unless we are committed to the empiricist maxim that to be is to be perceived.

If one maintains with empiricism that every reality is a phenomenon, one would of course have to deny the existence of the noumenon, and all *essentially* secret springs of action with it. The loss of this kind of cause transfers the causality of our actions wholly to a

6. *A Treatise of Human Nature*, bk. ii, part iii, sec. ii.

multitude of externals which could be construed as causes. What may not be explained in terms of the effects of one's own past actions, those of others, changes in the weather, and so on? The problem is to know where to stop; all the processes in the universe must be having effects on us to some degree.

All such external causes could well be called contributory causes, but there is nothing amongst them all which emerges as final or decisive, at least as long as we adhere to the phenomenal aspect. Without the interior or noumenal cause in oneself, which Hume recognizes as far as its action is concerned, the cause of our actions could equally well be called everything and nothing. Hume contends that liberty of indifference,[7] if admitted, must destroy the causal connection between the agent and his actions, in which case he could not be held responsible for them, whereas free will is normally invoked to *establish* moral responsibility. His conception of a soft determinism is therefore said to support morality and law, but this support only seems to extend to the connection between the action and the agent's state of mind at the time of the action. Moreover, if this connection is indeed necessary, as is usually accepted in any case, can that fact have any bearing on the question as to whether the agent is the originator of what is caused by him, or whether he is merely relaying the causality of some other agent? Hume's affirmation that responsibility does depend on the causality of the agent does not address the question as to whether the person's causality is intrinsic or extrinsic.

One may question the value even of this for morality and law, however, in the light of his earlier denial of the unity of the person,[8] which would make it impossible to say what his conception of causal necessity was connecting our actions with or deriving them from. If the person were not ultimately a unity, it would be hard to see how there could be any such thing as moral responsibility, of course, but in that case Hume's care to prove the necessity of human actions must also be in vain. We should be left with the conclusion that the real author of each of "our" actions was the disposition or

7. *Treatise*, bk. ii, part iii, sec. ii.
8. *Treatise*, bk. i, part iv, sec. vi.

passion which happened to be in control at the time, given that there really was no self or "we" to have had these passions.

In this case, responsibility for an action would only be traceable to a phenomenon with only a short, or even momentary, existence, and never to a complete person. This may be consistent empiricism, for if to be real is to be the subject of sensory observation, the unity of the person clearly could not be real, since it underlies all observables, whereas "his" individual mental and emotional states obviously are observable. But as there is no way of administering rewards and punishments to states of mind, we cannot accept Hume's disclaimers that nothing subversive of morality is intended.

The Unity of the Person

Hume further states in the same place that our impressions "have no need of anything to support their existence," though no attempt is made to prove this, (an objection to it will be advanced later), and we are never told whether it is part of the definition of an impression that it should be conscious of other impressions. In reality, there is nothing in impressions, like round, square, hot, loud, to suggest any such thing. The main conclusion here is that a man is "nothing but a bundle or collection of different perceptions, which succeed one another with an inconceivable rapidity and are in a perpetual flux and movement,"[9] and his idea of free will presupposes it.

This conclusion is of central importance both for empiricism and for Hume, such that what he says on most other subjects must be read in the light of it. It also makes clear why Kant found it necessary to establish a unitary self by means of the synthetic unity of apperception. If we really had to speak all the time of multiplicity, and not of unity or any unifying principle, such that all necessary connections subsisted only between fragments of experience, serious

---

9. Ibid. Hume's account of this subject, ending with the statement just quoted is remarkably similar to that of Cratylus, a follower of Heraclitus, who said one cannot step into the same river even once. (Aristotle, *Met.* 1010a, 15),but the effect of that on Plato led him to the theory of the eternal forms and the immortal soul. Thus opposite conclusions can be drawn from the same data.

logical difficulties must arise. One indication of this is the fact that
language obliges Hume to speak of "a" bundle or collection, because
plurality can only be conceived insofar as it is a single thing. Empiricism ignores the fact that unity and plurality are not a pair of equal
opposites, between which we can choose as we please. They are in
fact closely related, but only in the quite different manner which
recalls the relation between dependent and independent variables in
an algebraic function like $Y = X^2$. This peculiarity of unity and plurality is expounded in Prop. 1 of Proclus' *Elements of Theology:*

> For suppose a manifold in no way participating unity. Neither
> this manifold as a whole nor any of its several parts will be one;
> each part will itself be a manifold of parts, and so on to infinity.

Without unity, every plurality simply dissolves into other plurali-
ties in a vicious infinite regress, and the final result is nothing. The
consequence of this for multiplicity is that it presupposes unity and
derives from it, whereas unity has no such dependence on multiplicity. The relation between them, although not reciprocal for this
reason, is therefore indissoluble from the point of view of the multiple. Every multitude necessarily proclaims the existence of a hypo-
static unity. This relation between unity and multiplicity is reflected
in that between mind and matter, as the latter instances the former
relation. Mind is the center of the unity upon which the multiplicity
of material things depends, and, as with the former relation, mind
can theoretically exist without matter, but not vice-versa, at least if
it is to be matter as we know it.

A manifold as such cannot assert its own existence; something
must first confer a unity on it to enable it to communicate. This
applies, whether it is seen in terms of the separable soul according
to Plato, or of the synthetical unity of apperception according to
Kant. For this reason, the very multiplicity of our experiences is
the best proof of the unity of the knowing subject, the very opposite of what Hume thought it meant. The belief in a unitary personal identity is therefore not set up just to rationalize moral
responsibility, but for the more metaphysical purpose of accounting for our ability to take cognizance of multiplicity.

The cause of moral responsibility is not much furthered by

Hume's claim[10] that reason alone can never produce any action or give rise to volition, almost as though it were too manifest to require proof. This, if true, gives grounds for denying that reason could ever prevent any volitions, either. Thus no action could ever be either rational or irrational in itself. However, the difficulty here is with the major premise: why may one not carry out a piece of reasoning which could give rise to action? If by reasoning on evidence one concludes that gold exists in a mountain, that will arouse the desire for wealth, which in turn will cause the necessary action.

Diverse Causes of Passions

It seems reasonable enough to maintain that "Nothing can oppose or retard the impulse of passion, but a contrary impulse," but everything depends on the origin of these impulses. There is nothing to prevent a conclusion of reason from supplying one of them, if, as just observed, it too can arouse feelings. Thus the mind does not function in a set of watertight compartments, with different functions like reason, sentiment, and memory, each working with a sort of chemical purity. It is more a case of things essentially different working in combination to form a continuous whole. This is why there are not good enough grounds for the idea that only passion can act on passion, reasoning on reasoning, and so on.

Some passions arise from nothing more than chance events, while others arise from new insights, whether derived from reasoning or from perceived wisdom. It is really hairsplitting to say that reason cannot oppose passion, on the grounds that it does not comprise anything passional itself, when in fact it has the power to summon any number of passions according to its judgements. Hume's argument in this regard is as much a *non-sequitur* as saying that a general can do nothing to halt an enemy attack because he does not fight in frontline trenches himself.

One may feel anger which reason can show to be irrational, and this knowledge can be enough to induce a contrary passion, which would be natural in view of our fear of losing our hold on a faculty

10. *Treatise,* bk. II, part III, sec. III.

on which we rely in so many ways. In this sense it does take a passion to drive out a passion, while each passion is nevertheless qualified through and through by its causes, for which reason Hume's statement would be either simply untrue or a statement of the obvious. The curiosity which might make us look at the sun will never be as strong as the fear of damaging our eyesight in the process, and yet this restraining passion is not the result of a perception of an object, like the sun, but results from our reason's connection of the brightness of the sun with the limits of our eyes' capacity, and the fear of exceeding it.

In short, passions can be aroused by the mental perception of fields of possibility, whether for good or ill. Reason is one of our most important occasional causes of such perceptions, whence it is also indirectly the cause of passions expressive of its determinations. Other causes of these mental perceptions include chance encounters, actions which have unexpected results, and exchanges of information, but reason is the one which most directly depends on ourselves. It is rather its effectuality, not its ineffectuality, with the passions, which is too well known to need proof.

We should then be justified in classifying passions as rational or irrational, depending on their provenance, and conflicts between them are the inevitable result of the incompatibility of their causes. Reason's deduction that some work needs to be done may give rise to a desire to do it, which would be a rational passion, whereas any passion conflicting with it, such as laziness, would necessarily be an irrational one, from the fact of its opposition. Likewise, a rationally-based conviction that one was in the wrong may be opposed by one deriving from pride asserting that one was in the right, and which would be irrational in the same way. If I am right in maintaining that a passion can be aroused by the light of reason, this manner of distinguishing among passions will be valid. As if anticipating this answer, Hume has resort to his idea of "calm passions", so as to create the impression that all motives can be comprehended under the heading of passions. However, this idea is only notional and can scarcely claim to be practicable.

In regard to the argument for the impossibility of a truly irrational passion, concluding with:

'Tis not contrary to reason to prefer the destruction of the world to the scratching of my finger,[11]

it would only be reasonable to assume that this universal destruction should also engulf this finger and its owner. In that case, the contention would really be that it was not contrary to reason to prefer one's own destruction to a minor injury; this would seem to reflect the spirit of Hume's argument. But if the premises upon which one weighs the undesirability of the minor injury are no different from those on which one weighs that of the major injury, one will be left with the contradictory proposition that one could rationally want a greater amount of what in principle one does not want. If the major premise is "I do not want injury," I cannot opt for a greater amount of it in place of a lesser without negating my premise.

It is similar with regard to the question of preferring one's own lesser good to one's greater, granted only that it be part of our definition of the good that it is that which we desire. In this case, one's admission of the desirability of the lesser good commits one to a commensurately greater desirability of the greater good. This is subject only to the restriction that the good in question must be a good in relation to oneself in all the degrees under which it is considered. Otherwise one could include under the heading of "good", many degrees of wealth, power, leisure, and so on, which were greater than one was able to use in a way conducive to one's happiness.

In view of this limitation, one may rationally prefer a lesser degree of a given good to a greater, because the (objectively) greater good is not a good *in relation to oneself.* This, however, does not affect the objection raised above to Hume's argument, because that does in fact relate to both one's own greater and lesser goods. The relevance of this point to moral responsibility appears in the fact that the choices of greater or lesser goods for oneself cannot be separated from corresponding choices on behalf of other persons. If the one is as rational or irrational as the other, were it for self or others, there could be no intrinsic principle in us to which the moral value of our actions could be referred. If we could always choose a "lesser

11. *Treatise*, bk. II, part III, sec. III.

good" for others as well as for ourselves without irrationality, there could be no rational basis for moral responsibility.

However, this negation of responsibility will be unfounded if the above objection to Hume's argument is seen to apply. It may be argued that Hume did not intend the denial of moral responsibility as is alleged here, but it should be remembered that a philosopher does not have to tell his readers things which they can deduce for themselves if they only follow his arguments as far as he offers them. What we have considered in Hume are denials of common sense as radical as anything to be found in metaphysics, in the shape of arguments that there is no difference between human volition and natural causes; that the personal subject or self does not exist; and that no action can be rational or irrational in itself, such that the choice of the lesser good could be as rational as that of the greater. Taken together, the tendency of these arguments is, I think, unmistakable.

Kant's Response to Hume

Having considered moral responsibility in the light of a philosophy which is a source of arguments inimical to it, and having offered some counter argument to it, we may now briefly consider a philosophy which is wholly supportive of it. This treatment will be mainly based on Kant's *Groundwork to the Metaphysic of Morals*. Starting with the observation that the only thing which is good without qualification is a good will, on the grounds that all other kinds of good can be put at the service of evil, Kant argues that there is a fundamental difference between actions done from moral principle and those done from natural inclination.

It is argued that if nothing more than the personal welfare of the individual were involved, man would have need only of instinct. Reason, it is maintained, has no necessary connection with personal happiness, since its judgements have no regard to the wishes of the individual. Thus man must have the faculty of reason for some purpose which transcends the individual, and this purpose is to have a directing influence on the will, capable of causing it to be a good will. Although this goodness itself is not defined, reason is its judge and criterion. It is also indirectly defined from the argument that a good will cannot combine with other motivations so as to make the whole bad.

However, these arguments are affected by the strictness of our definition of happiness. What is said about reason and happiness is true enough if it is the kind of disinterested reason applied by the philosopher, but not if it is the kind of reason which is applied to the invention of new wants and to increasing the number of ways of satisfying them. To exclude the latter, one would have to conceive happiness in a strictly objective form, apart from the subjective sense of it, with which it is normally associated. This argument is therefore restricted in scope by basing itself on an idealized conception. Even the argument that the good will can never give rise to anything bad in combination with other things ignores the fact that "conscientiousness when united with intellectual error may lead to results that are simply deplorable,"[12] according to Sir David Ross. Ross does argue, though, that no complex of character is ever actually made worse by the presence of good will in it, though for this to be true, the goodness would have to be understood to include practical benevolence, because if it took the form of conscientiousness alone, it could simply have the effect of making someone more obedient and efficient for the kinds of activities demanded by totalitarian states.

Kant, however, does not seem to believe that a sincerely moral will could run into such errors. He would accept as real only the first two of four possibilities which arise here, namely, actions done from a sense of duty, and which conform to what duty requires; those done from inclination, but which conform to what duty requires; actions done from a sense of duty, but which happen to conflict with what duty requires; and actions neither done from a sense of duty nor meeting its requirements. Of these, the fourth would be real, but irrelevant, while the reality of the third would hardly be admitted. Possibly Kant is thinking in terms of the view that even unwitting error may still be rooted in some vice in the intentions, which makes them incomplete. For example, one may forget other

12. *Kant's Ethical Theory*, First Section.

people's birthdays, but not one's own, and mothers may drop crockery but not their own babies. This contrasts with Plato's view in the *Laws*, (see Chapter 4) where he says that an action done with good intentions is right, even if its results are harmful.

However, Kant gives a partial definition of the good will in terms of duty,[13] not charity, and the dutiful will is seen as a quality necessary for an imperfect being who would otherwise be ruled only by natural inclination. As the good will operates under conditions which are adverse to it, it is dutiful insofar as it overcomes them. Part of the reason for this is that Kant equates Biblical charity with beneficence performed from a sense of duty, and not with any affection for those in receipt of it. This is because actions are the kind of thing which can be commanded, whereas feeling or "pathological love" is not. If scripture is to be taken as a command therefore, it must relate to what consists in action. This does not exclude a natural inclination to this kind of action, but it does deny it a part in the definition.

Duty is also represented as the necessity to act out of reverence for the law. The idea of reverence in this connection is to be explained as a combination of fear and interest. The fear is liable to arise from our practical reason's imposition of a law on us and the awareness of the guilt which would result from its being broken. At the same time, there is the realization that this law is not merely imposed on us, but rather arises from the constitution of our minds. This sense of the law's being in some sense our own naturally inclines us in its favor, and the union of this inclination with the fear of law as such results in what Kant calls reverence. As only actions done from a sense of duty are held to have any moral value, this reverence gives the motive power to moral behavior.

Kant's view of duty and moral worth is criticized by Ross on the grounds that he does not take account of the need for dutiful behavior to have something in which to begin and from which to grow. Thus kindly actions done not from duty, but just from inclination, are the most likely starting point for actions tending increasingly to be based on duty, as they are the means of our first getting to know

13. *Groundwork*, chap. 1, 398.10.

what duties comprise. Also related to this question is the fact that it can always be in some sense possible to call an action morally good in regard to the second of the four basic possibilities, that is, on the grounds that it would be a fitting manifestation of a morally good will, whether there was one or not. Such actions might better be called morally appropriate, but Kant was not interested in this aspect of them, because to judge actions by their results would be to lapse into an empiricism-based utilitarianism which he was determined to transcend. This is why the purpose of the action is not counted, only the maxim it is based on; only something essential to the inner state of the moral agent could satisfy the requirement for an *a priori* principle.

But unless we had observed a number of instances of actions which had beneficial results, it would be most unlikely that we should ever concern ourselves with finding an inner principle for them. Such actions are therefore an indispensable bridge from actions of no moral value to moral actions properly so-called, and Kant is mistaken in speaking as though the latter could spring up all by themselves. While it is natural to consider first the material purposes of actions, and turn from thence to their formal principles, the reverse process to this is almost unheard of.

What Kant says concerning the inner motives or maxims of action can nevertheless be quite justified in itself, and the absence of insight into the external forms of moral value is probably no more than the result of his desire to concentrate on the essential.

However, more must be said in regard to moral action as manifestation of our consciousness of law, because if it should be an externally-imposed law, the maxim resulting from it would necessarily be contingent and natural, and therefore useless for the purpose of discovering a purely *a priori* source of moral action. Were it a law imposed by society, it would have no power to explain the meaning of morality, as it would be just a matter of convention on this basis. Even if it were a law imposed by God, nothing would be essentially different in this respect, because it could not be morally right simply because it was imposed by God; it would be imposed by God because it was right. But that leaves us still with the question as to what exactly is the right.

Ruled by One's Own Law

This law must needs be imposed by the moral agent upon himself, therefore, and here again it must not be imposed as a matter of caprice or even personal choice, but must result from the intrinsic nature of the agent. The manner in which this must happen would be analogous to the way in which man's forms of intuition impose the principles of space and time on all his sense perceptions. Just as space and time antecede all our perceptions, so the moral principle must antecede all the acts of our individual wills. At the same time, the manner of the imposition of the latter differs from that of space and time inasmuch as, on the one hand, we cannot at all escape spatiality and temporality in our perceptions, while on the other, we are not necessarily bound to obey the moral law when we act, even though it too arises in a non-empirical and therefore *a priori* manner.

This circumstance has also significance from the point of view of free will. To say the moral law is "imposed freely" is not really a contradiction, because its "imposability," the very possibility of its being imposed, is indeed a fundamental necessity, because the reception of the moral law under the form of cooperation rather than coercion is the only way in which it could be received without its *a priori* quality being lost. Short of this, it would still be a law, but would then be only a natural law, not a moral one, that is, not the kind of law which would be applicable to beings whose minds and wills transcend the material properties of the natural order.

Here, then, is the reality which inspires us with respect or reverence, and which has been explained on the basis of its twofold aspect, namely, as law inspiring fear and, as pertaining to ourselves, inspiring a proprietary sense, uniting fear and interest. This sentiment is the connecting principle between the conceptions of the mind and our outward actions. It serves much the same purpose as does the spirited or irascible principle for Plato, which is able to ally itself with reason so as to give it power over the desiring principle, which it could not have by itself on account of differing too deeply from it.

The presence of a mediating principle of this kind is an implicit admission of the traditional idea of man as a threefold unity, that of reason, sentiment, and sense. Some such idea seems to have entered into the general scheme of the Critiques, which was to study man and his knowledge under the headings of Sensibility, Understanding, and Reason, but the differences between Understanding and Reason were never developed sufficiently to make the ternary division effectual. This indicates that Kant is not very willing to follow through this conception, but for the present subject he is obliged to allow for it by reason of the fact that "thought of itself moves nothing," as Aristotle observed. There must be something between the mental and the physical by which they can interact which is prefigured in the universal triad of Being, Life, and Intelligence. The vital principle does in fact share in the properties of both the mental and the physical.

Moral responsibility can thus be seen to result from the connection between knowledge of the moral law and action by means of a certain state of sensibility which is subject to our will to a degree comparable with that of our thoughts. But this does not show us what the moral law is in itself. Kant takes it for granted that it is one thing only, and I think rightly, because a plurality of sources of moral goodness would only raise the question as to whether a given action was right according to all, or some, or to just one of these sources. Even if this were possible, good actions would still differ in their degrees of goodness, and would thereby be reduced again to instances of some common principle, which would remain obscure. Consequently, moral goodness must be established by a single principle or not at all.

This single principle is that the moral action be able to be made the pattern of a universal law without contradiction. Appended to it is the further condition that the action be not only logically possible as a universal law, but be such that we could also will it to be so. Thus one could will that everyone told the truth, but not that everyone told lies, because in the latter case, there would soon be no point in lying, and indeed no point in human speech itself, whence the contradiction in the action is manifest. The value of this principle is understood to lie in its immunity from all empirical or natural factors.

Limits to the Imperative

However, there is a discrepancy between the metaphysical immunity of this principle and the conditions peculiar to all particular actions. Actions are by their nature physical things, none of which can enjoy the status of an ideal identity, like a Platonic form. Consequently there is no such thing as either "telling truth" or "lying" as paradigmatic realities in practice. On the contrary, each separate action forms part of a larger whole of relations, by which its essential character is inevitably modified. This last point is important because it introduces an element of imprecision into the subject to which we are applying a paradigm like the categorical imperative, and this must lessen the precision with which our *a priori* principle relates to its subject matter, as a precise relation requires the same quality in both *relata*.

This objection applies in general, but it is not necessarily always serious in practice. There are innumerable particular cases in which telling a lie approximates sufficiently closely to lying-as-such for the *a priori* principle to apply strictly enough to it. In such cases, there is nothing in the motives of the person lied to which could make him unworthy of the truth, and there is no question of the liar being himself a victim of some deception about the meaning of his action. This action of lying could then for practical purposes be said to be unmodified by its relations, and therefore come under the rigor of the test of universality.

On the other hand, we can see where exceptions will arise, if we take one of Kant's own examples, that of a man A who pursues another, B, intending to murder him, and where B takes refuge in the house of C. A demands to know of C whether or not B is in the house. In this case, Kant maintains that C is bound to tell the truth to the would-be murderer, just as though this were a case of a paradigmatic lying-as-such. But this is precisely the kind of case where the modification of the character of the action by its relations is a significant factor, and therefore must set a limit to the applicability of the imperative. By not recognizing any such limit, Kant's argument leads to conclusions which are opposed to practical common sense, which nearly always takes account of someone's worthiness to be told the truth.

This is a weakness from Kant's own point of view, because he intends his principles to confirm the common sense ideas or innate moral sense from which they take their point of departure. Nevertheless, it is only a question of certain limitations which are not great enough to remove the essential validity of the theory. The basis for the conception of moral responsibility it provides is still of the greatest importance without having all that Kant claims for it. No paradigm, however important, can be expected to apply exactly in every case to things in the phenomenal world, but that is no reflection on the paradigm, and the categorical imperative is no different from all other forms in this respect.

It is enough that in the general case freedom and moral responsibility should result from the autonomy of reason itself, through which the individual is able to act more or less wholly in accordance with its principle. The intrusion of motives of any other sort than those of reason is something within our power to distinguish, and hence something for which we are responsible. Reason is the connecting thread through what has been instanced from Plato, Plotinus, and Alexander, and Kant, where they treat of free will, but man's possession of reason is not more significant than the fact that his use of it is anything but automatic.

6

Some Modern
Free Will Arguments

Real Minds, Real Agents

What I have said about free will in the previous chapters involves a number of assumptions which appear to be perfectly natural, but which are not shared by those who are influenced by linguistic philosophy. I have not tried to deal with this issue so far because those for whom linguistic philosophy is a commitment do not accept argument in support of conclusions of substance. They replace argument with ordinary usage, and treat logical necessity as a human or social convention. But for those for whom this form of thought is not a commitment, and who think that the rational point of view must be reckoned with, I will add some remarks which will clarify the position of these ideas in relation to it.

The case for free will can appear to be undermined by linguistic criticism, especially where the philosophical position depends on the assumption that the words it uses relate to objective realities or universals. For example, it was always taken for granted that minds were objectively real things, substances in their own right. Linguistic philosophy denies this, and would rather say that "mind" is merely a general term used to denote certain kinds of behavior which are conventionally attributed to minds. In this case, there could only be free will in the trivial sense of people doing things they like doing, and not in the sense of being the real authors of their actions.

The best answer to this denial of the reality of mind is to meet it on its own level with a denial that there is any such thing as *sense perception.* If the mind's own knowledge of itself is not enough to verify its existence, there is no reason why our interior experience of sense perception should suffice to prove that to be a reality either. Moreover, one's denial of it cannot be over-ruled, because the only tests to prove that another person has sense perception necessarily involve the use of one's own sense perception, and so would obviously be question-begging. This shows that the problem with denying the obvious as a strategy is that it is too easily emulated, not requiring any great ability, and this makes it too vulnerable to the same kind of attack.

Free will requires not only real minds, however, but minds with wills which have an effective agency to govern the person's behavior and choices. Needless to say, the reality of this mental agency is often denied in today's mental climate. One way of answering this objection is to propose a question to those on both sides of the issue: to ask those who believe in mental agency to say what they think would happen to the thoughts and manner of life of a person in whom this agency ceased, and to ask those who deny agency to say what they think would happen to a person if mental agency were to be implanted in him. The pro-agency side of the issue has an easy answer: all the thoughts and actions of the person would become purposeless and manifestly random, in a way no different from insanity. Conversely, the anti-agency side has no meaningful answer. Its advocates can only say either that the entry of agency will make no difference, or that it will make a harmful difference to the person involved.

If they say it makes no difference, they tacitly admit agency, because it could only make no difference to a being in whom agency had already been effective. A different variety of the same thing would now be acting, that is all. For example, if I take a vitamin supplement and it makes no difference, that can only be because I already had an adequate vitamin intake.

Besides, if the entry of agency made no difference, the anti-agency side would have nothing to object to. But in fact they do object, and that shows that they know it to be real, whether they admit it to be so or not. If it were supposed that this agency made no difference because it was really nothing, that could only be the case if the idea of mental agency was self-contradictory. But clearly it is not self-contradictory, excepting only the trivial case that agency is defined as a property of material things only.

Their other alternative, that this implanted agency *does* make a difference, and a harmful one at that, could only be an admission of the reality of mental agency, and it is they who fall into self-contradiction. On either alternative, then, agency must be real, in which case the fundamental condition for free will is valid.

Determinism is Incoherent

In *The Ghost in the Machine,* Arthur Koestler quotes an interesting paper on the subject of free will. It examines the hypothesis that free will must be untrue on the grounds that a complete set of data on a given person including all their mental states, knowledge, beliefs, emotions, strengths, weaknesses, and so on, would completely determine everything this person would do. One day, computer technology may be able to verify this, and so finally confirm this argument for determinism. Koestler goes on to argue the consequences of the fact that all these personal data must include the fact that one does, or does not, believe in free will.

My treatment of this is to apply the data-collecting argument to two persons, Smith and Jones, in a case where Smith did not believe in free will, but Jones did. In this case, the total information content of Smith's brain must include the fact that he does not believe in free will, and the total information content of Jones's brain must include the fact that he does believe in free will. Since we are presupposing the non-existence of free will, it must follow that Jones' belief in it will not have any effect on his behavior.

Two consequences follow from this. The first is that a complete set of conscious data about a person is apparently *not* necessary for us to know enough about him to be able to predict his actions, since we could omit Jones' belief in free will without reducing his predictability. Possibly, therefore, only some items of what we know, believe, love, hate, fear, and so on, need be necessary for prediction to work. The second follows from this, namely, that some beliefs can have no causal power in regard to the person who holds them.

This contradicts our initial assumption that all such mental characteristics *do* causally determine our actions.

This raises the question as to why anyone should say that a belief in free will can have no effect on one's behavior. One could not say in answer to this that it must be so because determinism is true, because such thinking would obviously be circular. In short, there must be some *intrinsic* reason as to why a belief in free will (*and* a disbelief in it) can have no effect on one's behavior. The one who disbelieves in it cannot be any more determined than he already is, just as the one who believes in free will cannot be any less determined. (This is so as long as we ignore the question of a subjective determinism, i.e., one which would be true for those who believed in it. In such a case, the belief in determinism would be the sole cause of one's determined behavior, whereas the present hypothesis is that of an unconditional determinism arising from the whole of one's mental contents).

On this basis we cannot say that a given belief is "not true", because it must in any case be an effective cause as much as any other which was true. The belief in determinism which determinists would call "true" should have as much and as little causal power as any of one's other beliefs.

These two beliefs, the one for and the other against free will, are in a very special category because they have a potential effect on, or relation to, everything one ever does. Thus they are not like beliefs as to what kind of material the moon is made of, and yet, though they pervade everything, one of them may still have no effect on our behavior. Depending on the circumstances, the will can be affected by almost any kind of belief, but the present argument centers on the supposed reality of beliefs which *necessarily* act of themselves on the will. Unless there is some way of defining such causally effective beliefs, however, this supposition cannot be presented with any probability.

The determinist case only looks strong as long as we can assume (a) that *all* mental properties have some effect on the will, and (b) that we can obtain a complete set of such properties for any given person. The above considerations show that neither of these premises is true.

Some Modern Free Will Arguments

The implications of the above conclusion that some of our beliefs have no effect can be shown as follows. Supposing I find some option very difficult to cope with, but, believing in free will, I fight against my negative feelings until I eventually manage to do the task in question. If the theory that this result was predetermined is true, my belief in the freedom of the will would have been one of the factors by which the determined result was realized. If this were the case, could there be other cases where we must believe the exact contrary of a given truth in order to confirm the truth in question?

For example, can one climb a mountain while believing this to be impossible for oneself? Can one cope successfully with an intellectually-demanding task while believing oneself to be unable to understand it, or telling oneself one can understand it when in reality one cannot? Even if the answer could be "yes" to these examples, we still would not be able to go so far as to say that we actually had to believe the ascent to be impossible and the work incomprehensible in order that we might do them at all. Yet, *mutatis mutandis,* this must be the case according to determinism. My belief in the freedom of my will must have had as much or as little determining force as any of my other beliefs. If it was effectual, then my belief in free will confirms my free will, but if it and other beliefs are ineffectual, determinists would have no source or cause for the determination they believe in.

It might be objected that, while the beliefs that the mountain could not be climbed and that one's mind was inadequate were both as contrary to the actual state of affairs as belief in free will is supposed to be, they are both negative beliefs, while the belief in free will affirms something positive. Can there be some other positive belief which is necessary for a given activity, despite being completely false? Suppose someone a hundred years ago believed the end of the world was near, and did penance for his sins accordingly, so as to die in a state of grace. Could we say that he could not have repented, unless he had believed the end of the world to be at hand? Obviously not, because many people repent without any such belief to prompt them.

Here again, to conform to the determinist treatment of free will, it must have been necessary for him to have believed in the end of the world in order to repent. But we know that this is not intrinsically necessary, even for him. Similarly, someone may wrongly believe that the prices on the Stock Market are on an upswing, when in reality they are starting to go down. If he acts on his mistaken belief and buys shares, he will soon be disappointed by the results. His false belief undeniably made his enterprise a failure. This obvious conclusion is very significant in relation to free will, since it shows that the falsity of a belief really does negate the action which results from it.

On the one hand, anyone can pursue a project to completion in the belief that he or she has free will, and still make a success of it. On the other hand, nearly every example of a relevant false belief, whether it be positive or negative, has the effect of subverting the activity and leading it to failure. This is only right, since truth and reality are inseparable, but contrary to this, the arguments of determinism must mean that we do *not* need to know all the truths relevant to our needs in order to act successfully, if a false belief in free will can be followed by a practical success. That flies in the face of nearly all experience, and would reduce truth and knowledge to mere options, or even to irrelevance. This shows that determinism denies the necessity for truth, reducing it to a psychological condition, rather than a part of objective reality. It thereby takes away any reason for thinking determinism to be the truth, because it denies the effective distinction of mind and external reality by which things can either be true or not.

Why Predictions Fail

There is an argument the original form of which was devised by Karl Popper, according to which determinism cannot be based on prediction, even were all the factors liable to cause our behavior known. Suppose it were possible to make a complete computer scan of someone's brain which detected every detail of its functions, which could be interpreted in terms of behavior. Applied to any given individual, it should then be possible to predict exactly what he is going to do next if our behavior depends on physical causes. However, he cannot be told what has been predicted, because as

132

soon as he knows it, the pattern of brain phenomena on which the prediction was based is radically altered in regard to the period of time in question.

Since the original pattern of brain phenomena has been altered, the prediction based on it can no longer be correct. However, the brain of the same person could be re-scanned, and a new prediction produced, but the same problem would arise again, as soon as he was told what it was. This leads to a vicious infinite regress, so that a prediction of a conscious being's actions is inherently unattainable if he is allowed to participate fully in the experiment.

However, the prediction might be made as before, but kept secret, while the subsequent behavior of the subject was observed. (Even this is an admission that only a very fragile certainty is in question). But the experimenter cannot guarantee that he will keep the secret, if only because he does not know the future. He would need to be able to predict his own behavior in order to be sure he would keep the secret, and as soon as he knew the answer, this knowledge would subvert itself in the same way as with the first prediction, since his mind would be altered by it in a similar way. Even supposing the computer prediction that he would not keep the secret was kept secret from the experimenter, it would undermine the certainty of both predictions, because they must now be known to a second experimenter who has made the brain-scans they are based on. He in turn does not know whether he will keep these secrets, and his silence (or not) would have to be predicted in the same way, leading to an infinite regress of experimenters.

These views on the problem of secrecy are unsatisfactory, however, because the premises of this kind of experiment are not made clear. In fact, the main premise is that of a world of ultra-high technology with unlimited powers *to invade secrecy*. To be able to read the contents of someone's brain would be just about as far as this could go. This gives another reason why the experimenter cannot know whether he will disclose the prediction or not. In a world with this invasive technology, there is every reason to suppose that those whose actions were predicted in this way would be able to find out what had been predicted about them. When the experiments on their brains had been done, they could go home and use their own super-computers to hack into the experimenter's super-computer and find out the prediction for themselves.

That would surely be easier than scanning a brain. If this piece of hacking had been part of the content of the computer's predictions about their subsequent actions, as it well could be, the utter vacuity of the whole attempt to prove determinism in this way would be obvious: it would be predicting its own failure. In short, there is something self-contradictory in the idea of a causal determination ruling the actions of conscious beings.

Nevertheless, it would be a complete mistake to conclude that if actions are freely-willed they cannot be approximately predicted or predictable in many instances. Insane behavior is unpredictable, and there is no free will in that. Actions which are always predictable and actions which are always unpredictable, as in the insane, are equally devoid of free will, and this is what reveals the complexity of the idea of freedom.

If it were the case that freely-willed actions were always unpredictable, it would mean that no one would ever be able to achieve any purpose if it had to be done in stages. For example, the creation of a garden, the painting of a picture or the making of a piece of furniture involve sequences of activities all of which are, broadly speaking, predictable, or at least reliable in a general way, though not in particulars. Besides, in most activities, the more focused and effective the will is, the more its activities will be predictable or at least reliable. Reliability is a form of predictability which is indispensable for morality, which is the focal point of free will. All such cases of effective will are naturally understood to be prime examples of free will in action, not of physical determination.

Conversely, if the will was always predictable, both in general and in detail, it obviously could not be free, because such results are obtained from artefacts which have no free will, or will, at all. Thus it must follow that free will must be predictable under some conditions and unpredictable under others, and the proportions of predictable to unpredictable instances must be both endlessly variable and completely unpredictable. That is where the unpredictability criterion truly comes into its own in connection with free will. On this basis, free will is able to comprehend the widest range of realities, including

134

both determination and indetermination by being something more than either of these two by itself. On the physical level, determination and indetermination are hard alternatives, but in the realm of the spirit they are rather complementary. That is why there is no point in trying to think of God as exclusively and unreservedly "free". There is no freedom without the power of determination.

Too seldom is it realized that "absolutely free", if it is not self-contradictory, is synonymous with "absolutely without moral responsibility," which is a strange thing to attribute to God in view of the commitment to morality which the Christian religion and most other religions must have. It could only be true of the ever-laughing gods on Olympus, doing things to mortals for their own amusement. However, in view of the foregoing, it can be seen that there are adequate reasons for thinking that absolute determination is as impossible for conscious beings as absolute indetermination.

No Free Will, No Intelligence

One consequence of the denial of free will is that this denial itself, along with all other beliefs and affirmations, is predetermined for us by external forces. It would therefore not really be our own, because, whether we claim that there is or is not free will, the statement we make could not be the product of our individual intelligence and will, because one's mind could only be the transmissive medium connecting our behavior with its real cause. In this case, we could not say anything because it was true (even if we believed that to be the case), but only because we were compelled to do so. Subject to our usual assumptions, any such origin of speech would falsify all statements at a stroke, and the denial of free will would be both false and self-contradictory.

If someone tries to convince us about a certain matter, and it is found that he is being paid to do so, we assume the idea to be untrue. Similarly, if his motive were some other material factor, like fear of danger or loss from not trying to persuade us, we also assume the assertion to be unworthy of belief. But if there were no free will, all statements would be of this kind, as natural forces would rule without exception. We only take seriously statements which we believe to come from a genuine effort to see the truth for oneself. In this case, determinism would deprive us of any grounds for belief in, or even interest in, things said by other persons.

It may be argued that our interest and belief would also be determined by the same forces as those which determined the words we were listening to, but that only deepens the futility of what is going on. Even though the sense of futility were imposed on us as well, the fact would remain that even our deepest motives could be thenceforth nothing of the sort. This means that there is a fundamental difference between having no free will while not knowing that to be the case, and having no free will and knowing that we have none. That in itself is a problem for determinism, since it cannot determine whether or not we know that it rules us.

Nevertheless, it is still possible that denials of free will may not really be false, because it is possible that the statements "There is no free will," or "Determinism is the truth" may express the truth, even though they were imposed on our minds by natural forces. After all, "Two twos are four" is just as true if it is uttered by a parrot or a tape recorder as when it is consciously uttered by a rational person. Our individual exercise of intelligence could then be illusory while the things it was made to state were true all the same. The converse of this is the case where a statement expresses a genuine act of intelligence while still being untrue. That could be because the reasoning was based on false premises, or on inappropriate ones. The mere fact that truth and freedom of utterance are thus separable at either end of their relation shows that we need to consider the consequences of their separation a little more closely.

The external control of what we take to be intelligent thought has major problems of its own. If it is the universe or nature which causes all the things we think and say, and not our own mental faculties, we need to explain why there is so much conflict, why people argue and contradict one another. Is there more than one universe or more than one order of nature? In any case, there is only one universe of which we are actually a part, and therefore only one by which we could be controlled. Besides, natural laws do not admit of exceptions, and apply equally to everyone, which one might expect to result in harmony, or at least compatibility.

Some Modern Free Will Arguments

The action of only one determining agent need be considered here. If our wills were the puppets of a number of such controllers, either those controllers would be acting with free will or not. If they were, there would be no reason in principle why we also should not have free will. If they were not, and they were all controlled by just one power, they would be mere transmitters of that power, and we would be subject to this one power along with them.

As things are, a single natural order or determining power constantly contradicts itself through those whom it compels to speak, in which case it is causing the utterance of a great deal of untruth. That undermines our hypothesis that the things we are predetermined to utter in this context could nevertheless be the truth. Why should "Determinism is true" express the truth when so many other things we are made to say do not? And can the same cause produce contrary effects? There is in any case a serious flaw in the idea that the utterance of truth could be predetermined in all cases. This is owing to the fact that we naturally assume that the word "true" in this predetermined context must have the same meaning as it has when it is applied to the thought of minds which are believed to be free to judge. In reality it does not and cannot have the same meaning.

When we exclude the idea of the mind with free will, the idea of truth may not mean anything at all. The ability to pronounce a statement to be true or false is irreducibly individual and personal. If it should somehow be determined by external forces, "true" could obviously not mean "true in the judgement of the person who takes it to be so," which is what we normally take it to mean. So what could "true" mean in a deterministic context? There could be no answer to the questions: "True for whom?" or: "True on whose authority?" The word would have to have a meaning so different in this context that there would be no reason to use it. In this case, there would be no ascertainable truth as we understand it, and therefore no intelligence in the absence of anything to which it could relate.

Conversely, given free will along with intelligence, the attainment of truth is possible, though never guaranteed, but without it, it is not even possible. Therefore the affirmation that it is true that there is no free will is, after all, self-contradictory. This conclusion is also of wide application to all systems of monism or non-dualism, which similarly involve a rejection of intelligence. The presence of intelligence or truth in any being can only be verified by another intelligent being. Where there can be no "other" being of any kind, intelligence and truth have no meaning.

The Bifurcation of Nature

This bifurcation is experienced in the fact that if one can perceive any object, one can also form a mental image of it. This is the most basic function of the imagination, and because of these images, everything in the outside world is duplicated for us, and here we can find a sound basis for free will. Since every external object to which the will can relate is thus two objects, one physical and one mental, there is apparently nothing to compel the mind and the will to relate to either of them more than the other. As a matter of constant experience, we can devote time and attention to an external object and to our image of it in any proportions we like, even to ignoring either of them for the sake of the other.

Here is one of the fundamental indeterminations in the natural order on which the freedom of the will is based. In ordinary experience, the amount of attention paid to the images of things is relatively small, whereas it will be much greater if one is a poet or a novelist. If in fact our choices between attention to objects and attention to their images were somehow determined by unknown means, we ought at least to know from what quarter the determination came. Attention to physical objects may be caused by the relations of our bodies to the physical world, of course, but what of attention to their images? Physical causes could not impel us toward something fundamentally different from them and still remain strictly physical.

Conversely, by the mental agency or causality of the will, we can attend to external objects just as casily as to mental ones. There is an asymmetry here, but not an inconsistency, because the external object is known to us only by the image of it formed by the senses, and this image retains the same nature when it is thought of in abstraction from the thing which naturally causes it. Thus for mental causality, the difference between the two categories of object is purely relative. The mental forms with which we perceive an objectively real sunrise are the same as those with which we conceive an imaginary one. On the other hand, the idea of purely physical causes inducing us to attend to mental images rather than to the objects they derive from is to require that a given kind of cause should produce an effect radically different from itself, rather as though darkness should produce light, or random collisions logic.

The options of being determined by the external object or by its mental image, or by a combination of both of them rule out any scientific answer, because science has to confine its reasonings to physical causes alone. Our actual unhindered mobility between these two radically different kinds of cause is what makes our freedom a reality. As time passes, all the things we experience by the senses are matched by the mental images we have of them, which is to say that man's experience could be said to move forward along parallel tracks, neither of which is able to monopolize his time and attention if he does not want it to do so.

The "double life" implicit in this means that we can engage with things while standing aside from them, or go abroad while staying at home, as A. O. Lovejoy put it, and so deal more effectively with the same things when we return to them. For example, an engineer who could only work physically on a machine would be far less effective than one who could work mentally on his ideas and images of the machine as well. Constant immersion in practicalities is never practical in the long run. The use of this universal bifurcation is the key to the freedom and power which mankind has in relation to the rest of creation. Anti-dualists who wish to deny this possibility in favor of a monistic or "single subject" idea of the self are really teaching a preference for the intellectual impotence of the animals.

In particular, all originality and creativity would be excluded and discredited if the duality of object and mental image were to be denied. To be able to make intelligent changes in the world is for those who can stand back from it and engage with images of it. All rational forms of action require the overview of externals which can only come by means of images, and from thence comes free will and moral responsibility. Here, it is possible to see why physical or natural causes cannot act directly on the mind or will. The physical cause or agent is never known or experienced until the mental faculties form their representation of it. While that is happening, a change of category takes place during the transition between the natural cause itself and our experience of it. As a result, the physical cause now exists in an additional and different mode, and only thus, in its mental form, can it affect us causally—or not—in a way which involves the will. But that is precisely not physical causality.

However, besides experienced causes, or experiences liable to be causes, there is still the supposed possibility that our wills are determined by things we never experience at all. Determinists and Christians are both liable to maintain some such thing for different reasons. Were the operations of the will (not its bare existence) directly caused by God, it would mean that God was either unable or unwilling to create a being with a real will of its own, and neither of these alternatives is worth defending. If it is caused by agents other than God, there would be a question as to how many of them there might be, and of how far are they consistent with one another.

In fact the idea that free will is really determination by some unseen agency amounts to a denial of rational thought, because to make the unknown a part of one's reasoning is to make ideas incoherent, including the idea of unknown agents. This is because the category of the unknown is quite big enough to include even more agencies which could restore or preserve freedom, so revealing its futility as a basis of argument.

In reality, the belief that our actions really are caused by our wills is just as well founded as the belief that we exist. To say that one's will is the effect of another will is thus literally on a par with the contention that one's identity is really that of somebody else. All arguments which require the denial of immediate evidence must at very least produce other kinds of immediate evidence to replace it with, and that is hardly ever possible.

The Excess of Causes

To amplify what I have said about the excess of causal agencies over effects actually produced by them, it can be seen that if there were no such excess, and the relation between them were always one-to-one, something essential to causality would be denied, namely, its transformative and irreversible powers. If there were a one-to-one relation between the number of causes and the number of effects, it would mean that the action resulting from any such cause was limited to the level of a change of location or of other external relations. True causal power is not just that of producing a certain effect, but also of producing it despite the actions of adverse forces which tend to prevent it from doing so. Without that condition, the idea of causality would be trivialized to insignificance.

An example of this can be seen in the case of an institution, like a college. If those who applied for admission to it were automatically accepted, there would be a one-to-one relation between causes and the effects they produced. In this case, the causality involved would effect nothing more than a change in the nominal identity of those involved, and if this were to be the rule, the institution could not survive because, qua institution, it must be able to differentiate itself from the rest of society. Without that, its own causal power would be nullified likewise. The excess of potential causes over actual effects implied by the selective function is thus the condition for there being real causal power in practice, whence it follows that *causality implies exclusion.* If, for example, I will option A, I must reject options B, C, D, and so on, and if B, C and D are not possible alternatives, my choice of A must be a non-event (a one-to-one causality), and cannot properly be called a choice at all. In other words, my will would not have exerted any causal power; hence in this case it was not a real agent, and therefore not free.

This implies that causes are very unequal among themselves in regard to power and content, whence the necessity for causality is matched by its lack of any systematic or monistic control over nature, and such is the basis upon which free agents can operate. This causal exclusivity has an aspect of disorderliness, but its positive relation to order appears from the fact that its tendency is opposed to the rise of entropy, because reductive processes work most freely where causes act in a disordered manner.

On this basis, free will does not require any denial of causality, but rather demands it. When it is applied to the continuity of substance, it can be seen that the continued existence even of a physical object exemplifies the principle of causal exclusion because any such object is subject all the time to mechanical and chemical pressures (i.e. potential causes) which, if allowed full scope, would soon render it unrecognizable, if they did not destroy it altogether. In reality, natural bodies normally have properties which are able to nullify most of the destructive agencies they encounter, at least for certain lengths of time. Such stability and continuity thus results from the causal exclusion principle referred to already, showing that it causes the absence of change as much as change itself.

Whether causality is in static or dynamic mode, the common factor between these two modes is that natural forces obstruct the action of a certain group of causal agencies and give free passage to only a few or even only one of them. This selection and rejection of causes by natural means goes on all the time, so that where the human will acts in like manner it is making no difference to the fundamental pattern of natural causes. While the natural order is not violated, it is redirected in such a way that its processes can attain the most intelligent results, namely those which instance archetypal realities of an order which is never attained by nature left to itself without human intelligence. The rigorous selections and exclusions of potential causes is the basis of such highly-formed possibilities, whereas the action of cause without a directing and unifying agent produces only strife, confusion and decay.

In living organisms, this negative pattern of causality appears in disease and mortality, and does so most clearly where the immune system is damaged or destroyed. The latter example is a clear example of failure of the causal exclusion principle as it occurs in living organisms, along with its entropic consequences. The functions of exclusion and selection among causes are intimately involved in the very possibility of existence for individual beings, whether intelligent, or animal, or inanimate. The metaphor of 'Maxwell's Demon' is a personalized version of this same process of causal selection and rejection. It has been used as a hypothetical way of explaining how the entropy or disorder of a system might be lowered. But its activity of intercepting molecules and diverting the fast-moving ones to one side of a partition and the slow-moving ones to the other side is something which lies outside the realm of purely physical causes, since it requires the act of an intelligently discriminating will. It shows that the true source of order is mind and not nature alone.

The short-range idea of causality implicit in the above, which was first considered in the context of Plato's *Timaeus*, is one which is open to free will while not denying the conditions necessary for a scientific understanding of nature. Besides being constantly confirmed by experience, it is an alternative to, indeed a denial of, an earlier view of natural causality according to which the universe was wholly made up of unbroken chains of cause and effect which all extended from its beginning to its end. This idea of causality, if true, would certainly rule out free will, and it is the reason why many philosophers have argued for determinism. However, this idea is not scientific, and never was, because it consists in an imaginative extension of all we know about cause and effect far beyond the reach of experiment. It is therefore more truly a scientific myth, one which was inspired by the way in which Newtonian mechanics was found to apply to the seemingly never-ending movement of the heavenly bodies. Thus a kind of cosmic romanticism was born, which fostered an idea of universal causal rigor which did not serve to explain anything, while it excluded some of the most important possibilities in those who believed in it.

Reversal of Entropy

While using two essential arguments for free will, I did not make clear the relationship between them, although their full effectiveness only comes from the combination that can be made of them. I have used the argument that each one of us is beset by a multitude of potential causes, each one of them trying to make us do things incompatible with what would be caused by most of the others, e.g., some to make us work, others to make us take it easy. Clearly they cannot all win, and in the event our will opens the door to one and locks the doors on all the others at any given time. This means that whatever we do, it will be possible in principle to show, after the event, what causes gave rise to our action, but it does not mean that this causality was able to make us accede to it. On the contrary, our will has, as it were, a "casting vote" to allow the action of some causes and block that of others. The contention that "everything must have a cause" has therefore no power to establish determinism, being true only in a sense which is trivial in regard to the will.

However, there remains the possibility that the selective agency of our will could itself be a natural force, and so be determined by causes not clearly known to us. How to save it from this criticism, and show that the rational will is superior to natural forces, while nevertheless directing them?

In fact the necessary answer to this question is given in the Conclusion, but without drawing attention to the connection. The problem is to show that our rational will is capable of something that can never happen among natural forces. To find this, we turn to a law which governs all physical systems without exception, whether physical, chemical, or biological. This is the Second Law of Thermodynamics. We need only show that our rational will can act contrary to this law, therefore, and we can be sure that its choice among natural causes will itself be unconditioned by them, and so must be truly our own. This is to be seen in the fact that we can spontaneously create order, whether it be to write an essay, a verse, or a tune, or simply to set playing cards in numerical order in their suits (i.e., something which cannot happen by chance alone).

The order we thus create is almost *gratis,* i.e., it does not involve any remotely comparable amount of destruction. This contrasts completely with the natural order, where the Second Law ensures that every new ordered structure, such as that of vegetable and animal bodies, requires for its nutrition and growth the destruction of more ordered matter than is realized in the new growth. This is no more than what is implied by the constant rise in entropy universally on the physical plane. Consequently, our elective agency is not a force on the same level as that of natural causes, even though it is close enough to them to determine which of them shall operate and which shall not. In other words, when our rational will makes its choice among the different causal series incident upon us, it does so from a position ontologically superior to them. Our ability to reverse entropy is also proof that our own agency is not, in such instances, at least, a part of natural causality.

Some Modern Free Will Arguments

Soul as a Power of Self-Motion

This property is the key to the soul's ability to lower entropy, and spontaneously create new order. The idea disclosed here is an example of this. Because all other movers in nature are themselves alter-motive, it is necessary that they must eventually use up the energy imparted to them, and fail. Such is the reason for the universal downward tendency to disorder in the realms treated by physics and chemistry, and this is what a self-motive being is by definition exempt from.

There is a necessary connection between rising entropy, i.e., the tendency toward disorder, and the inability to conserve motion which has been imparted from without. This continual and inevitable lessening of motion means, among other things, that nothing in the material world can remain the same. The importance of the idea of soul as self-mover can be seen from the way in which it was rejected by Aristotle, because this idea so clearly goes beyond purely natural forces; Aristotle wanted to naturalize everything.

The acquisition of motion from without obviously implies that it is taken from other beings if it does not arise internally from the soul. This implies an essentially competitive condition in relation to available energy, which is clearly in accordance with the Second Law. Conversely, the power of self-motion means not only at least a relative independence from external sources of order and energy, but an ability to sustain order and thereby to act with free will. Clearly there could be no such thing as free will if the soul were not self-motive.[1] This may not have mattered to Aristotle, but it should have mattered to Aquinas and his successors. It is interesting that free will *per se* was not of enough interest to Plato for him to give attention to this issue, despite what he wrote about self-motion.

Otherwise put, the presence of self-motive beings must be excluded by the Second Law from every realm to which this law applies. Conversely again, if we ask what, if anything, could escape the Second Law, the answer has to be, a self-motive being.

---

1. Concerning the soul and self-motion, see also R. Bolton, *Person, Soul, and Identity*, Chapter 1.

The souls of animals must also have self-motion, but that does not mean they can conserve or create order. The self-motion that has been discussed above is self-motion combined with intelligence. Without the latter, the self-motion would have no rule of its own to guide it to results which would be any different from those of the biosphere in general. Thus it is with the animals. Their lack of an individual ruling intelligence means that although their motion is self-generated, it cannot differentiate itself from that of all the alter-motive phenomena of its environment. The Second Law might well be redefined as "the Law of alter-motive natures".

Aristotle rejected Plato's conception of soul as the self-motive principle, and his idea of the soul was later adopted by the Scholastics in response to historical change. This change in the idea of the soul, as far as it is valid, corresponds to the finite nature of the power of self-motion in human beings, in regard to how much can be effected with it, and its further limitation owing to the usual moral and intellectual deficiencies of those who employ it. A certain pragmatism is manifest in this, because the idea that the essence of the person is the soul and that the soul is a self-motive being is necessary for a fully spiritual idea of the self, no matter how inconvenient it may be for social purposes.

Those who have challenged the Platonic idea of the self are able to make a case for doing so because their alternative tends to make people more aware of ways in which they are dependent, and so be more attentive to their moral needs. But if this is believed to be more necessary than the higher flights of self-knowledge, one should remember that it can take a toll which most people would object to if they understood what was involved. This takes various forms, as where the more passive idea of the soul means an unnecessarily-increased sense of one's own mortality, which is an obvious source of religious unbelief. Besides that, the added sense of dependence results in a reduced ability to resist the unspiritual fashions and passions which infect society, whether today or in the Middle Ages.

These penalties imply a lack of free will, of course, and in ages of faith, when the higher possibilities of free will are more frequently realized, they are counteracted by more prayer and more devout practices, but in times when faith recedes, the naturalized idea of the self does all the harm it is capable of. The result is a spiritual wasteland, analogous to the material wastelands left behind by defunct industries.

My use of Platonic ideas for the purpose of arguing for free will was appropriate because this philosophy contains so much which is conducive to the idea of free will. In the first place, there is the idea of the soul as having—and being—essential self-motion, with its argument for personal immortality, whereby death could only mean the departure of the soul when the body was no longer able to correspond to its moving force. The idea of self-motion necessarily implies that the soul or self must be capable in many cases of acting without input from any outside cause. In view of this, it is inconceivable that Plato did not believe in free will.

Besides this, free will requires a one-way relationship between the agent and his surroundings, because he must be able to act without being acted upon, at least in certain cases. For most philosophies, this idea of a one-way relation is questionable, if not self-contradictory, but for Platonism it is not only acceptable, but forms part of its essential metaphysic.

Consequently, an essential idea for free will is in constant use there, where it appears in the *eidos*-instance relation. The *eidos* is wholly causal in relation to the instances, but the latter have no effect at all on the *eide*.

Platonism's idea of self-unity is also important in this connection. The unity of the soul differs from that of a material object; in the object, the unity is simply an imposed order instantiated in it, and therefore, on relations among a multitude of distinct elements, whereas the soul to some degree actually is the form of Unity, which it comprises along with all the other forms, by means of which it can identify both the forms in their own realm, and in their material instances. (At the same time it falls short of pure unity, because it has a diversity of functions, though not of parts, and these functions being diverse in themselves, the degrees of activity in them will also vary with time.)

According to Platonism, the soul thereby has at first-hand all the properties which make for concreteness, which the material world has only at second-hand. Every positive quality of material things is thus owing to the presence in them of some *eidos* or other in accidental modes, whereas the soul has it essentially. On this basis, Platonism guarantees the soul's power to act upon material things, as being something more, not less, concrete than they.

The presence of *privation* in nature, and the action of causes *per accidens* both weaken the continuity of causes, and so make it possible for causal processes to interpenetrate one another. This also means that the will can intervene among them without violating causality as such. This discontinuity, or disarticulation among causal processes also arises from their being only instantiations, and not their *eide* or originals. Platonism can therefore be said to support for reasons of its own the Aristotelian view of nature as permeated by a real non-being which was employed effectively by Alexander of Aphrodisias, as we have already seen.

Conclusion

The Limits of Causality

While the writings of the major philosophers emphasize the role of reason in regard to freedom, they are nearly always content that thought should be free to follow the laws of reason, no matter what natural laws govern the body. They hardly ever proceed from this to a full application of the idea that rational processes must take place in a realm to which natural causes have no access if they are to be accepted as true, although Plato and the Platonists evidently assume something like this in their doctrine of the separable soul which, as Proclus says, "reverts upon itself."

Before going on to outline any theory as to how our will can be able to change physical reality, we should note in passing that in practice this possibility is never doubted for a moment, no matter how little understood. Man is a teleological being through and through, and there is not a government department in the world without a commitment to some form of *planning*, that is, the belief that consciousness and will can change the outside world in accordance with purpose. Either man is a natural product of the universe or he is not; if, as evolutionists think, he is, his teleological behavior must be simply a continuation of that of the universe, and there would be no grounds for denying teleology in nature as a whole or for denying free will. Conversely, if he were a special creation, placed here by God, that might make it possible to say his purposeful behavior was not due to nature as such, only in this case man's free will could still be real even were there no teleology in nature.

A thoroughgoing doctrine of free will does in fact require that there be a certain duality in the world-order, even though subject to the unity embracing the person and the world. While the primary duality is between the material and the psychic, there is a secondary one within the material world itself, in regard to two different levels of causality. This latter distinction is necessary because, without it, there could be no working connection between the order of contin-uous causal necessity as studied by science, and free wills which are by definition exempt from such laws. It is therefore a question of the natural order itself giving rise to an intermediate causal state in which the same causes still operate, but only in short, broken, and disorderly sequences. The continuity of nature at this causal level would then be due only to the broken sequences all beginning and ending within other finite sequences, and not to the existence of unbroken causal chains.

This possibility can be explained on the basis of the production of planets from the causal system of the universe as a whole, where continuous causal chains really can exist in the vastness of space, where the motion of stars and planets and the evolution of stars from hydrogen continue over enormous periods of time without interference from extraneous causes. On those planets where solid, liquid, and gaseous states of water coexist, all physical and chemical processes act in such profusion and in such close proximity that none can act long without interruption by others. This state, which is conducive to the existence of life, is what I call "discontinuous determinism", because while all its separate parts are subject to causal necessity, the whole has a fluidity which comes from the fact that causes are constantly appearing and disappearing because of changing conditions.

This pattern of nature may be schematized thus:

Continuous Determinism (Uninterrupted causal laws)	Material Objects
Discontinuous Determinism (Fragmented causality)	Living organisms
Freedom (No physical causality)	Rational Agents

Life, and the discontinuous determinism it is based on is the mediating principle between the realms of mind and matter. It does this by partaking of some of the properties of both, and this does not give rise to an infinite regress, because discrete *relata* can form a continuum, as where quantities like a^2 and b^2 are joined by the mean ab, in which case a^2, ab, b^2 are continuous in terms of the quantities in question. Likewise, the natural numbers 1, 2, 3, 4, ... are continuous in terms of unity. However, there need be no doubt that continuous determinism governs the universe as a whole, especially when one adds the extensions of it like gravitation in the terrestrial world. But given the above modification of causality which is typical of most of the earth's surface, we have conditions under which agents who are not intrinsically subject to natural causality can interact with the physical world. The broken-chain causality involved here is of a kind adaptable to the action of free agents.

Mind as Cause

This still leaves the question as to how interaction between the physical and the psychical can take place, though the difficulty here varies according to the kind of philosophy applied to it. It is possibly least difficult in terms of Platonism, for which the psychic principle is the primary reality, possessing *in potentia* everything which is deployed piecemeal in the external world. When soul acts, therefore, it does not act on the utterly alien, but rather on instantiations of its own essential principles. There is a parallel with Kant on this issue, because it was Kant's conviction (though proof was not thought compatible with it), that the power of the rational will to act on the external comes from its being the thing-in-itself, which lies at the heart of the reality of all phenomena. In Platonic terms, it could be said that here Kant is preserving the *eidos*-instance relation, while denying the conscious insight into the eidetic reality claimed by Platonism.

This approach eases the problem one would otherwise have with the concreteness of the world and the abstractness of thought. On Platonic, and possibly Kantian, principles, the agent partakes of the essence of what it is that makes the world concrete. The conception of man which results from this is that of the microcosm, an ancient idea which has received support from modern philosophy of science in the form of the Anthropic Principle. The proven ability of human intelligence to penetrate to the inmost structure of the atom, and the lack of any inherent barriers to its advance, argues for man an objective cosmic centrality of which the Ptolemaic system was a symbol and an anticipation. Although Kant nowhere refers to it by name, the conception of man as microcosm also plays an essential part in his philosophy, since for him man is in himself the embodiment of the Forms of the Intuition and the Categories of the Understanding, which give form to all the content of the external world.

As an epitome of the essential cosmic principles, human nature can be expected to comprise the three broadest subdivisions of the world, those of Material Object, Living Organism, and Rational Agent. These are also the states based respectively on continuous and discontinuous determinism and freedom, according to the scheme above. By means of this conception, continuity between the different states of the universe is ensured, with the interposition of discontinuous determinism; this gives the necessary counterpoise to the concomitant requirement that the world should consist of such deeply different realities as the material and the psychical.

On this basis, the establishment of freedom does not imply any need to deny the reality of causal necessity at its own level. This is also the manner in which freedom is treated by Proclus in his *Providence and Fate;* fate is accepted there, though not as ruling universally, while the true destiny of the soul is to become conscious of, and actualize, the nature peculiar to it which transcends the fatal order to which it has been joined by nature. The relation which the rational, or free agent has with the natural or fatal order is far from simple because, on the one hand, he must be able to act causally on it, while on the other he must be exempt from it *qua* rational agent, at very least during the time for which he acts. He will, of course, be subject to any amount of causality from it in regard to his physical, sentient, and emotional states, but his reason alone cannot be subject to any such causality without its at once ceasing to be itself.

This implies that the free rational will must, if it is to be effective, have a one-way relationship with the natural world, though that may seem almost contradictory. How much difficulty this involves depends again on the school of philosophy to which it is related. For the Platonic metaphysic of *eidos* and instance, all relations are of the one-way kind as a matter of course, although this expression is not normally used of it. Thus the *eidos* of triangle-absolute is the formal cause of all particular triangles, without itself being in any way reciprocally affected by the presence, quantity, or duration or anything else about the particular triangles. Just as all causal power goes unilaterally from *eide* to instances, and perhaps from noumenon to phenomena, so the causal power of the rational will has but a single direction insofar as it is rational.

The Platonic conception of the soul as rational agent requires that it should do in a vital, variable, and dynamic manner what the triangle-*eidos* referred to above does in a uniform and immutable manner. That it should do so is implicit in the doctrine, and it is remarkable that this conclusion has never been explicitly worked out by the great philosophers, while it has been done by C.S. Lewis, albeit in a book intended for a popular readership.[1] Because of its non-specialist orientation, the presentation of this most important idea is not as rigorous as it might be. One important mistake in it is Lewis' acceptance of the determinists' premise of nature wholly under continuous causality, a sort of causal seamless garment, which his conception of free will had to keep making holes in, so to speak. Thus he gave hostages to the opposition by allowing free will to be the source of an insoluble dualism between natural causality and the will's causality.

This idea of nature effectively rules out free will, although it is by no means a consequence of the uniformity of nature, according to which the same causes always produce the same effects. However, uniformity implies nothing about either the durations of causal series, or about how many of them must come into operation at any given time. Thus it is in itself of no use for determinism, which has to supplement uniformity with a gratuitous homogeneity of nature, by which all causes would have the same continuity of action as those which apply to celestial mechanics. Lewis failed to see that any such idea of homogeneity was not logically implied by uniformity and was in any case a restatement of the position he was opposing, and so weakened the case for an idea of fundamental importance.

1. *Miracles.*

Many other thinkers have also been misled by this unwitting extension of uniformity into homogeneity, as the distinction involved has not attracted much attention in scientific thought, then or now. Little has been said of the contrast between the continuity and precision of causal processes under ideal conditions and the erratic patterns which they follow on the terrestrial level. That the orderly mechanism of cause and effect is always at the mercy of the most disorderly of things, namely its ambient conditions, is a matter of constant experience, and rules out any supposed homogeneity. An alternative to the determinist view of causality has already been given in what was said about the parts of the material world with which living organisms are in contact.

The realm of full necessity, or continuous causality, attenuates of itself under terrestrial conditions into one where the series of causes and effects are increasingly broken up by one another's action. This is accompanied by an excess of potential causal agencies, only a minority of which produce their effects at a given time. In this outer fringe of the causal order, therefore, the rational will does nothing unnatural when it acts therein as an additional cause, since interventions are possible from any direction, subject to discontinuous causality.

That the rational agent is not affected by the natural causes on which he acts can be seen in the way that the same reasoning can be reproduced with equal validity in the minds of different persons, despite the innumerable physical changes that take place in and around each person at the same time. The body and its surroundings are nothing but variability: external temperature and pressure, the composition of the bloodstream, pulse rate, humidity, position in the cycle between waking and sleeping, to name but a few. All these things are in constant cyclical variation, producing continual new combinations which can never recur. The presence, over against all this, of the conscious rational self, which receives and rationally interprets images of the world around it, is a matter of experience which evidently antecedes all its particular contents. Such is the self which can deduce identical conclusions of a logical nature, while the person as a whole may undergo any number of changes.

154

Conclusion

The Foundation of Values

Now that a number of arguments for the freedom of the will have been examined, it remains to relate this freedom to the wider context in which its implications are most clearly manifest, firstly on the political and cultural level, and secondly in relation to self-realization. I have avoided doing this in the previous chapters because it could easily appear that the great practical importance of its related issues was being offered as an argument for free will, which of course it could not be. If enough has now been said by way of argument, however, an outline of all that depends on the reality of freedom should remove any doubts as to the justification for a study of this subject.

Free will, to be real, must be the human manifestation of a primal freedom or indetermination in the essence of every person. In the realm of the spirit it is analogous to the free space around one's body, without which no physical action would be possible. Only by the indetermination of this freedom can our individual actions be truly our own and truly our own creation; such would be the "nothing" from whence we created them. Man's power to create his own inner and outer acts reflects God's power to create beings. This freedom in the core of the individual self is by definition exempt from all natural forces and conditions, and when thought and will proceed from this centre they give rise to actions which are qualified with the inner freedom of the self, so that the nature of the inner man is shared by the outer.

The place of freedom in the life of religion must therefore be assured, and it appears accordingly in the New Testament, as in: "And ye shall know the truth, and the truth shall make you free."(John 8:32) and: "For freedom God has set us free; stand fast therefore and do not submit again to the yoke of slavery." (Gal. 5:1) and: "Now the Lord is the Spirit, and where the Spirit of the Lord is, there is freedom."(2 Cor. 3:17). At the same time, the emphasis on chastity in Christianity shows its commitment to freedom in a practical manner. Nevertheless, what is said about it is restricted because it is too easily confused with the countless uses and abuses of freedom which lead to wrong-doing and eventually to the suppression of freedom itself. For this reason, some religions practically ignore freedom in favour of predestination, and the faith they require is not identified as an act of freedom.

In Catholicism, the nearest approach to this position is to be seen in the restricted idea of free will bequeathed by St.Augustine, enough for obedience perhaps, but not for much more. This has had a great deal of influence up to the present day in the West, whereas Orthodoxy does not inherit this problem with free will. Yet despite the suspicions caused by the morally dubious aspect of freedom, it continues to have an unfailing magnetism, such that sacrifices have always been willingly made for it, even by those who did not see themselves as particularly religious. However, a much more dangerous opponent of freedom lies in the equally universal desire for security, even though it comes from a much lower spiritual level when it is made into a primary objective. Freedom is all too often traded for an earthbound security of this kind. While security is legitimate in principle, since it is closely related to freedom, it is a good only when it is a consequence of some more essential value.

The absurdity of making security an end in itself appears in the fact that this means that we must believe that we will still be free to enjoy security when we have given up freedom in order to do so. On the other hand, a virtuous life creates its own kind of security, but in such cases security as such is not directly aimed at. In theory, the spirit of religion is no more than neutral in regard to desires for worldly security, but in practice the traditional religions, with their will to punish the heterodox and the unbelieving, unwittingly connected religion with a pursuit of worldly security and success in pre-modern times. Truth must be upheld and error rejected, of course, but the human consequences of that in the long term also have led to the downfall of traditional civilizations, even though not so rapidly as where the truth is not defended.

The use made by the Church of a widespread desire for security-first is the subject of Dostoyevsky's Legend of the Grand Inquisitor, a parable intended to show how religion is stifled when it makes use of means which exclude freedom. Some take it as an anti-Catholic story, but in reality the Catholic Church has always defended the values upon which the freedom and dignity of the individual depend.

Conclusion

This appears from the fact that the most militant heresies which the Church fought against in the Middle Ages were nearly always ones which denied the individual by trying to abolish the family and private property. (See *The Socialist Phenomenon* by Igor Shafarevitch).

To accept security in place of freedom always brings with it a loss of power along with the loss of freedom, because freedom and power are inseparable. While they are not the same thing, they have so much common ground that they can often be treated as equivalent for many practical purposes. Thus denials of free will, and therefore of individual freedom, are always an essential part of political programmes for reducing society to a mass of powerless units, who are thereby open to maximum exploitation. All power and freedom would then be the preserve of those at the top of such societies, which are necessarily anti-individualistic.

Under such political systems, the suppression of the individual is treated as an ideal, despite the fact that all the most admirable and valuable things in human life are the work of individuals working freely on their own initiative. Plato denied this, never noticing that he was thereby demanding the suppression of his own philosophy. The Microcosm is more than equal to the Macrocosm, though this is beyond the grasp of those who can only think quantitatively, which makes Plato's failure to understand it all the more strange.

The ideal of freedom is always liable to arouse hostility as a result of the ways in which abuses of it by some curtail the freedom of others. There is accordingly a literary tradition of tidy-minded idealism, starting with More's *Utopia* and Campanella's *City of the Sun*, which would prefer to make sin and crime impossible by taking away all or most of the freedom of the individual. Something approximating to this anti-ideal was achieved in the empire of the Incas. This was a case where the crucial connection between freedom and power proved fatal to this civilization. Its systematic denial of personal freedom made it impotent in the face of danger, with the result that an empire covering half the South American continent was destroyed almost without opposition by a mere two hundred Spaniards. There was nothing accidental about that, because freedom-denying cultures soon end up politically and morally rotten.

To take a recent example of this, it is barely twenty years since the implosion of the Soviet Union, which collapsed without even being physically attacked. The spiritual capital of pre-Communist times was finally exhausted. In the end, unfree collective entities can do little more than exist and feed. This is why the reasoning which supports free will is in accordance with the central place which freedom has in relation to all the values. It is also something other than a value because, without it, the values would be inoperative. I have already alluded to this where I argued that there could be no intelligence and no truth without free will. Love likewise depends on freedom as much as knowledge does, because it can only be itself when free of controlling or determining factors, and this indicates that neither love nor knowledge can be an ultimate reality by itself.

Christian tradition gives first place to love, while the Greek tradition gives first place to knowledge, but far from being opposed, they are inseparable because there is no knowledge without there first being a love of knowing, and no love without a knowledge of the loved. Consequently, it appears that pure love is no more possible than pure knowledge, despite what is taught by Advaita Vedanta and other forms of impersonalism. Just as love must be wholly one's own act, knowledge must be free from all causes except the causality of truth itself. Freedom is equally necessary for them both, and if freedom were a value it would stand in order above love and knowledge, but in fact it is not so much a value as a condition for values to be realized in practice, rather as the air breathed by living creatures is not itself a life form. There is also the comparison with the empty space needed for physical action.

The possession of freedom means that everything in human life for good or ill is a result of choice, regardless of how high or low a degree of free will entered into the choice, so that in this life the will is free even to subvert its own freedom. With freedom we may get better or worse, and achieve foolish objectives as well as wise ones, and this ambivalence further explains why freedom, for all its importance, is not strictly speaking a value. The condition for the realization of values is also the condition for failure to realize them. Throughout life, we continually make choices which mostly serve to reinforce choices we have already made, good and bad equally. This is the basis of the "self-creation" which results from the fact that our voluntary acts are our own creation. Such freedom brings a responsibility for being the way one is, because this self-reinforcing tendency of our choices makes the conditioning of our early life less and less relevant as life goes on.

Freedom for Self-Realization

An essential aspect of freedom is that of being able to do as one pleases, and this must not be lost sight of. Nevertheless, it has been subordinated to more metaphysical considerations because of the great complexity of human nature, which does not allow any simple answers as to what it is that one should wish to do. Man is an epitome of all modes of being, most of which are more or less peripheral in regard to what is most essential to him. For this reason, it is possible for his choices to be in accordance with any one of the many-headed multitude within him, such that the condition of doing as one pleases begs the question as to which modality of the being dictates the kind of activity in question.

Freedom is nothing if not the fulfillment of one's essential possibilities, and therefore it cannot consist in the fulfillment of possibilities which are shared with any number of other species. It may even be said that the least fulfillment of what is truly essential to human nature effects a greater degree of freedom than the maximum fulfillment in what is more or less accidental to it. This was the guiding principle in Kant's view of the purpose of human life:

> The ability to combine abstract notions and to master the bent of the passions through a free application of considerations takes place later; in some never in their whole lives; in all, however, it is rather weak: it serves the lower forces (instincts) which it rather should dominate and in whose mastering consists the excellence of his nature. When we consider the lives of most men, this creature seems to have been created to absorb fluids, as does a plant, and to grow, to propagate his species, and finally to age and die. He of all creatures least achieves the goal of his existence, because he uses his outstanding faculties (mostly) for such purposes

which other creatures accomplish more securely and conveniently with far inferior faculties.[2]

There is a certain asymmetry between the intellectual faculties and the rest of the personality, inasmuch as mind can always aid any number of purposes based on sentiment or instinct, whereas there is a realm in which mind and mind alone can suffice. The relation here among human faculties is a further example of the "one-way" relation referred to previously. Human beings, by being reasonable, know themselves to be such by reason itself, and they know their other faculties such as imagination and sense, by means of reason as well.[3] On the other hand, imagination, sentiment, and sense do not know mind, which is why they cannot strictly be said to know even themselves, as knowledge of images and sentiments requires more than these things themselves. This limitation of the outer faculties contrasts with the way we can know many things by reason alone, that is, things of which we could not form any imagination, such as a star thousands of times the size of the earth.

Therefore there is a one-way relationship between the intelligence and the lower faculties which manifests the hierarchical relationship between them. In this respect there is only a relative difference between the relation of the rational will to the other faculties and its relation to things in the outside world. The will is therefore free in proportion as it acts in accordance with the rational principle, because it is only with the latter that the individual is wholly a cause, and not an effect, through its non-reciprocal relation to nature in addition to the fact that the rational will which man freely makes effectual in this way is what is most essential to him.

In Platonic terms, the world is permeated by the ideal-forms twice over, firstly in the generally recognized sense of their being manifested in instanced forms, and secondly by man's psychical agency, in which the forms are all present *in potentia*, in a pre-instantial state in minds. Only by means of the latter is the union between the prin-

---

2. *Universal Natural History,* third part, appendix, p. 187.

3. Proclus, *Commentaire Sur La Republique,* tome III, 277, Festugiere tr., pp. 236–237.

cipial reality and the relatively unreal world completed. It is an entry of the most real into the less real, in a way which recapitulates the original instancing of the forms which constitutes the world.

True and False Freedom

This conception of free will, with its specially asymmetrical relation, gives a new insight into how an agent can operate both "on" the world and "in" the world. By adherence to his own principle and withdrawing himself from a passive relation to the world, he is in reality more effectively a part of the world than ever, but in a very different way. He mediates between the world and its formal causes, and confers a new degree of order on it, in a way which joins nature to the spirit.

Failure to secure this relation to the world leads to a false freedom which binds the will to the materially-real for its own sake, leading it into a metaphysical dead-end where its causal power can only dissipate among relativities. Thus human energies get merged with those of the natural order, with which they move down the common energy gradient of the universe in the direction of disorder. The alternative to this, which is argued for here, can appear too introverted and negative toward the world, in a way which may seem to be a result of bias. Nevertheless, it is only a matter of negation negating something which is deeply negative in itself.

In the light of what has been said in previous chapters, the will has a wide margin of activity, within which it may direct its energies more or less toward either material expediency or a conscious pursuit of values for their own sake. While both of these are inseparable from human life, there is wide variation in the possible proportions they may bear to one another. Secondly, it may be argued that a distinctive kind of self-identification results from the prevailing direction taken by this choice; the subject participates in the modes of being of these different kinds of object, with consequences for his sense of personal identity.

But the mode of being of the material world *qua* material is, quite simply, flux. Everything in it is raw material to be made into something else, from the moment it came into existence. If absolute materiality could be approached, it would be a condition in which aggregation could scarcely keep pace with dissolution. The human consequence of this is that identification of the will with its relations to the material world is an assimilation of the person to impersonal and irresistible forces of change. This need not be at once experienced as an evil, and it seldom is, at least up to a certain time. However, the essence of what is involved here is an assimilation of the self to an alien reality, which inevitably asserts its own nature at some stage, at the expense of the will which is joined to it when no change of direction is possible. This applies equally to individuals and whole nations. The negation of freedom does not actually arise at this point, but it rather emerges from what was firstly an implicit denial of it becoming explicit.

Such a deceptive semblance of freedom is possible as a necessary consequence of the material imitation of eidetic reality which constitutes the natural world. The captivity of the will by the laws of the natural order, and the resulting manner of life, is what is traditionally called fate. Conversely, the application of the will to the intelligible reality is to join it to a reality of like nature to its own, in which it will not encounter any ultimate negation or impossibility, and which is causal in relation to the fatidic order as a whole. That the will should thus be ultimately guaranteed against insoluble conflict means that it is free, both in the sense of doing as one pleases within certain limits, and in the sense of exerting an activity which is ultimately its own master. For this reason, a predominating pursuit of the higher values is the means whereby the individual can combine fulfilment both as a natural being and as a spiritual one at once, and enter a realm where the properties of nature and grace, material and intellectual, are reconciled.

Appendix:
Kant and Free Will

A Kantian Ambivalence

Much of what Kant has to say in vindication of free will is unfortunately counteracted by some of his other, more limiting ideas about it, which would make it seem reconcilable with a completely determined natural order, where the will could not change the course of events. He associated the latter point of view with the idea of each soul making an extra-temporal act of choice, which determined the course of the natural life of each person, such that the question of altering this course of life in the world could not arise. Such at least was his conviction, though he did not claim to know it. Consequently, if we are to hold to the other side of Kant's treatment of the subject and try to establish a free will which can manifest itself in practical ways, there will have to be some criticism of the idea of nature which underlies his work. The points made will then be referred to occasionally in what follows.

I think this can be done without criticizing what is essential to Kant's own conception of causality, if a distinction is drawn between the conception of causality peculiar to his philosophy, and the conception of it which he took over from the scientific thought of his own time. His acceptance of the latter was deliberate, because he thought that attempts by previous philosophers to reconcile God and free will with the new scientific idea of causality were unsatisfactory, as they required one to belittle the claims that science seemed to have the right to make for itself. It seemed to him that he could only construct a really convincing case for free will if he took as his point of departure the new science at its own evaluation, and then showed that free will could pass this acid test.

He denied that science had access to things in themselves, because it treated only phenomenal things, but that did not answer the problem it raised. However, his plan was not completely carried out, and his acceptance of contemporary scientific philosophy was to be the cause of conflicts in his work which still require resolution. Changes which have taken place in modern philosophy of science show that we have reason to be suspicious of Kant's science, because its outlook was founded so largely on the success of Newtonian astronomy, from whence it was uncritically assumed that the same causal perfection must extend everywhere else. If we can show that too much was granted to the claims of science after all, the resulting view of free will should be more true to Kant's real intentions than the opposite course would be, in view of the honoured place he gives to Freedom, along with God and Immortality, as the essential subjects of speculative thought, regardless of whether they could be made actually known.

We can admit with classical science that there are no uncaused events, without committing ourselves to the idea that there must always be a one-to-one correspondence between all causes and all effects. That indeed would exclude freedom, but there does not seem to be any proof for it. Rather, the evidence is for a superfluity of causes, among which there is very often no necessary determining factor permitting one of them to act while restraining the others.

When causes operate under special conditions, as in the laboratory, the one-to-one relation of cause and effect can be made to prevail, and determination can be as complete as required. Even under natural conditions it regularly occurs, but—and this is the important thing—never for very long under terrestrial conditions. When conditions cease to favor one kind of cause, the result is a new condition which favors one of the other potential causes, and which then comes into operation. In this way, the continuity of causality-in-general is never broken, while on the other hand, the particular causal sequences involved may be very disorderly as a whole.

This aspect of causality was apparently never considered by Kant, as he says in the Third Antinomy[1] that the objection to a separate causality by free will would be that "the laws of the latter (nature) would be continually subject to the intrusive influences of the

1. *Critique of Pure Reason,* A451, B479, Norman Kemp Smith, tr.

former (the will), and the course of phenomena, which would otherwise proceed regularly and uniformly, would become thereby confused and disconnected."

He assumes that the only alternative to sheer disorder is the steady, uniform application of particular causal laws, thereby conceding too much to scientific determinism. This clearly ignores the third possibility considered, namely that of a disorderly sequence of causal activities, each part of which is orderly and uniform as far as it goes. Since Kant's idea of natural causality is thus not the only one possible, it would be well to consider the alternative in a little more detail.

The universe as a whole can exist with overall continuity without there being any continuity in the causal chains of which it is composed. We need only suppose that the beginnings and endings of the separate series hardly ever coincide with those of others. If this view of causality is justified, causal power would reside just as much in its displacement of other possible causes as in producing the effect peculiar to it. Causality would then imply exclusion in nature in a way comparable to the way we know it does in ourselves, where the choice of A means the rejection of B, C, D.

On this basis, the difference made by the human will would therefore consist in the changes it makes to the relations between accepted and rejected causal forces, though for Kant there can be no direct causal connection between the Noumenon and the phenomenal world.[2] While the will has no power over causality *per se*, it can have much power over which of the different causal series shall continue, and which shall not, and which potential ones shall come into operation. Thus the will would not have to violate natural causality in order to change the patterns of the latter in ways that would allow a maximum of intelligently-directed order to be realized in it.

Causal Selection

Selection and rejection among natural causes often happens randomly by itself, but when it is effected by the will, it is a necessary

---

2. But the will, as we know it on the phenomenal level, can nevertheless act as a cause, whatever its relation to the Noumenon.

but not sufficient condition for new order to be brought into being, because the will must also be allied to an intelligence with some prevision of the result.

Any system, whether human or natural, in which causal selection and exclusion were to fail, would simply degrade. Were there no variety among the speeds at which the molecules moved, Maxwell's "demon" would have no causal power, having no basis for selection or rejection. There is therefore a close relation between free will and causality on this basis, and by no means any antagonism. A hubbub of voices all talking at once is an example of what happens when causal agencies all act at once without any selecting principle. The end result is much the same as if nobody spoke at all, and the simultaneous absence of both freedom and causal efficacy in this instance should be noted.

There are then two main ways in which the idea of causality proposed here differs from the classical form of it; firstly in that most causal series are judged to be short, because they depend on conditions which are never stable, under terrestrial conditions at least, and secondly in that there are in any case always far more potential causes than there are possible effects. It does not seem to be an analytic *a priori* conception, or a fact of observation, that every cause must give rise to its effect, in which case we are not bound to assume it in philosophy, however important it may be for classical physics. It might be objected that a cause which never produced its effect was not really a cause at all, but this line of reasoning gets harder as the examples get more concrete, as, for example, where one would presumably have to say that a seed which never germinated was not really a seed at all. Our constant observation of effects which dependably follow causes over short periods of time gives us no insight into how far this regularity extends into long periods. Moreover, no matter how many causes are found to be in operation, there is no way of defining a total of all the causes that *could* have acted, which implies that there are no empirical grounds for the causal completeness which Kant thought one had to accept.

That there is no fixed proportion between causes and effects is also evidenced by the universal evils of excess and deficiency. In whatever realm they arise, they are equally a threat to order and existence, and are obviously states of disorder, despite the fact that they are brought about by the workings of causality. Nevertheless, causality as a source of universal order has much aesthetic appeal, which along with its promise of power through knowledge of predictable events, may explain its widespread acceptance. But it is only in astronomy that this particular idea of causality seems to be factually well founded, so there is no point in trying to apply it to realms in which human life is directly involved. It is the more surprising that Kant himself did not reach some such conclusion, in view of his own assertion that causal laws would never suffice to explain such things as the growth of a blade of grass.

These considerations make a difference to the setting of Kant's philosophy, which leaves us more free to accept the arguments for man as a real causal agent than Kant supposed. Above all, it eases the problem of "spontaneous origination"[3] which was so serious for Kant, by its reduction of the element of continuity in natural events. In the Thesis of the Third Antinomy, it is stated that natural causality alone does not suffice to explain the appearances of the world, on the grounds that such an explanation cannot be achieved without the addition of the causality of freedom. If no such agency entered the flow of events at certain intervals, there would be no fixed points between which the causal processes could be thought to move. It seems to be essential to the idea of causality that there should be such sequences of finite length between termini, because without them, causality by itself can only refer explanation backwards in time, in an infinite regress, which would make causality itself all but useless. (Kant was too ready to accept this.) But exactly how such spontaneous interventions in the natural order can occur is not explained, because the then prevailing idea of nature did not allow for them.

In the same place, we are given the example that his decision to rise from his chair may depend solely on himself, and must form the beginning of a new infinite series of events. Had he postponed this decision, that particular infinite series would never have arisen, and another, rather different one, would have begun instead. This, at

3. See Third Antinomy, Observations, A448, B476.

least, seems to be the logical implication, and it fits well with the idea I have already put forward, that the range of causal potential in the world is far greater than can ever be realized in actual effects. At the same time there is no need to suppose any breach in the continuity of natural processes. Each decision to rise from the chair begins a new infinite series which flows directly from the infinite series by which he was seated there in the first place, even though it "succeeds" to the latter without being produced by it. This also is close to what I have already hypothesized as to how causal series can in effect break in on one another, whether by human means or in nature by itself, without lessening the hold of causality over the whole.

Kant's Account of Causality

But so far, the idea of causality has been taken for granted, and has been more or less a mixture of scientific and common sense ideas of it, whereas Kant developed a deeper theoretical idea of it, to which we must now turn before applying it any further. Kant's proof of causality starts from Hume's supposed refutation of it on empirical grounds, which reduced it to a subjective way of looking at things which merely followed one another in a certain order without any objective necessity. The practical need for the idea of causality was not in question, so Kant concentrates on the question of its origin, and rejects all attempts at an empirical justification of it.

He affirms the distinction between analytic and synthetic *a priori* judgements, so that by means of the latter, the truth of causality may be proved. Pure mathematics is the realm in which synthetic *a priori* judgements are seen to be valid, whence the whole problem is to show how their scope can be extended outside the bounds of mathematics. Kant thought Hume ignored this aspect of mathematics because he did not want his sceptical method to be seen to be in conflict with it.

Kant's solution to the problem was that our intuitions contain the "form of sensibility", which is a reality logically anterior to the individual person, and is intrinsic to mind *per se*, after the manner of the Platonic forms. Space and time are the fundamental elements in this *a priori* form of sensibility, from whence it can be seen how geometry is provable in regard to this inherent concept of space. But the problem then is, how does geometry become applicable to external spatial objects, and not remain merely a property of man *qua* man? The answer is that external realities themselves only reach our consciousness via this same spatial form of our sensibility, which exists as it were "between" it and them like a tinted lens between the eye and the world around it.

On this basis, the applicability of mathematics to things in the external world is necessary and indeed a foregone conclusion. This implies that we do not perceive things as they are in themselves, but only appearances of them. If the possibility that the thing-in-itself and our intuition of it according to our form of sensibility might both be equally relative to some third reality is excluded, the above conclusion would seem to be necessary. As the idea of causality itself is strictly confined to efficient causality in the realm of phenomena, we cannot even assert a causal link between the thing-in-itself and what we perceive, even though such a link may be possible.

The source of illusion is the understanding, not the senses. Thus the understanding may misjudge what the senses present in the appearances of a planet's forward and retrograde motions, and conclude that the planet actually does move in opposite directions. The phenomenal world, integrated with mathematics, is thus not in itself illusory. The laws of nature are determinations of the *a priori* forms of our understanding, and the resulting certainty of the knowledge we have of them obtains at the price of their being phenomena, and not things-in-themselves.

This certainty is one and the same with the objective and universal validity Kant ascribes to the natural laws, both of which terms imply the other. Subjectivism is avoided by referring perceptions to the single, identical nature of all human minds underlying all personal differences, thanks to which all can agree concerning the world they perceive. By this means, the distinction between Primary and Secondary qualities, as set up by Locke, is overcome. The Primary qualities are now as much a part of the realm of appearance as are the Secondary.

Perceptions are transformed into objective experience by their being "subsumed under the concept which determines the form of judging relative to the intuition in question." When the concept is that of Cause, the particular content is universalized. The concept of causality forms the bridge between merely perceiving a relation between two things, and being able to say that this relation must always hold good. Thus it constitutes the true temporal order of things, and overrules the imagination, which can relate the same objects in any order it likes.

However, causality is only one of the two most fundamental concepts of the understanding, since it is logically connected with that of substance, as shown in the third part of the Table of the Concepts[4]: "As to relation"—"Substance, Cause, Community." The understanding's concept of substance is put forward as the means of removing Hume's doubt, inasmuch as the problem of one thing's resulting from the existence of another is really inseparable from the problem of *subsistence*, namely, how successive states of one and the same being follow from one another; "that at the foundation of the existence of things lies a subject which cannot be the predicate of anything."[5]

Likewise in the First Analogy,[6] the permanence of substance is the basis of all phenomena:

> Only in the permanent, then, are the relations of time possible.... Substance in relation to time is thus another concept by which we construct our world. The idea of substance necessarily implies its permanence throughout time, and is the ground of the principle that "nothing comes from nothing," and its converse *"in nihilum nil posse reverti"* ["nothing can revert to nothing"].

Because of this concept, each phenomenon exists within the whole extent of time, past, present, and future. All things are unified in the temporal continuity of substance. We are able to represent all external existence to ourselves by means of it, and without it all separate beings would dissolve into instantaneous fragments.

---

4. Prolegomena, (303–304).
5. Ibid., (310).
6. *Critique of Pure Reason,* Schematism, B183, Norman Kemp Smith, tr.

Change concerns only the modes of substance, but the subject of change is unchangeable. The absolute origin or extinction of anything is inconceivable,[7] because such changes are never conceived except either in relation to a previous sequence, after which an existence began, or during which one ended. Substance therefore gives rise to cause, since the question as to how one state in one object A can give rise to another state in another object B is inseparable from the question as to how the successive states of A and B themselves give rise to one another, and how individual entities result thereby.

Causal connection is thus not a datum of experience, but is rather what makes experience possible, and what makes it capable of teaching us anything. Causality is logically prior to every generalized experience, just as space is in relation to every spatial object perceived. It is integral to the "mere form" of experience, and so enters into everything, whence it is a property of our experience of things and not of the things in themselves. This is why it is said that knowledge extends only to the experience of phenomena. Hume thought only in terms of ideas being derived from experience, but never vice-versa, and it is in this respect that the power of Kant's answer to his scepticism is manifest.

One-Sidedly Traditional

The success of this conception is largely owing to its being a revival (whether intended by Kant or not) of an ancient wisdom idea of man as a microcosm, the complexity of whose nature fitted him to be *capax universi,* as the Scholastics put it. The revival of this idea is nevertheless one-sided, in that one half of the original form of it is suppressed in Kant's treatment of it; the unique nature of man as the epitome of all things is retained, but not the objective being of all the essences to which the complexities of his nature corresponded. Thus for Kant man's complexity generates phenomenal reality instead of corresponding to it. Even so, enough of the traditional conception was adopted so as to break the force of empiricist

7. Ibid., A188.

scepticism, but not enough for it to be clear as to how much the new insight was indebted to the older forms of thought.

According to J. Pieper,[8] it was a favorite idea of the Scholastics, derived from Aristotle, that "*anima est quodamodo omnia,*" or that "the soul is in a certain sense all things." This property of the soul was what defined man as a spirit, inasmuch as spirit is the power to relate to the totality of being. It can be seen that Kant's philosophy, worked out according to the Transcendental Table of the Concepts of the Understanding, is in fact a detailed, even though restricted expression of the development of this idea of man, which was able to reassert itself amidst all manner of changes tending to obscure it. It belongs at the opposite extreme from the idea of man as a mere blank tablet, upon which data happen to inscribe themselves, an idea which is also perennial in its own way.

Thus when Kant speaks of his "Copernican Revolution" in philosophy, by which he internalized the basis of external knowledge, he was only breaking with a quite recent form of tradition, but not with that of Platonism, the metaphysic of which has always inverted the common sense order of objects and their universals in very much the manner of this revolution. Under either system, knowledge is only possible upon the transition from the individual entity to the universal form. For Kant, the concept of line, for example, must be "subsumed under the concept of magnitude," although the line, like all other particular things, is taken much as it is for common sense, and not as an instantiation of a universal which must pre-exist it.

Kant's doctrine makes the transition from instance to universal more difficult to understand than it is for Platonism, and the result is like that of a metaphysics which bases itself on a systematically restricted selection of universals. Only what are termed the "non-sensuous universals" are retained, these being such as cannot be manifest as individual instances or objects, and they are restricted so as to be part of the mind's own constitution, while being denied any objective status outside it. Thus on the one hand, man has a set of concepts as part of his being which form the system of all his

8. See *Leisure the Basis of Culture,* 'The Philosophical Act', chap. II.

synthetic *a priori* judgements, but on the other, the *a priori* truth of causality, among other things, is established without any objective basis in the thing-in-itself, or in any non-phenomenal principle.

The main reason for giving this account of Kant's vindication of causality, possibly the most powerful ever made, is to show that the strength of argument in favor of causality *per se* does not in itself add anything to the causal necessity to which we may be individually subject. This is because, before it can apply to us as individuals, the causal principle must needs be instanced in particular agents. Being thus discrete and separate, they then share in the contingency of the subjects they act on, which rules out the sort of monolithic and all-embracing causality that determinism would require.

The free will is said to belong to the world of the understanding, which is said to contain the foundation of the world of sense. Man is subject *qua* intelligence to the law of the world of understanding. But the main difficulty in discussing freedom lies in its aspect of negativity, inasmuch as it is known by a mere absence of constraint by natural inclinations and other natural forces, which we can at least have clear ideas of. It is therefore manifested by the indirect means of our being subject to the moral law, because it can be shown that moral principles could have no meaning unless we were free in our wills.

Moral Law from Free Will

In the *Groundwork*, though not in the *Critiques*, Kant presents this relation in the reverse order as well, by affirming that the freedom of the will can establish the reality of the moral law. This means that the conception of freedom must be further extended, so as to avoid a circular argument in this regard. Accordingly, a form of causality is attributed to it which informs or underlies the causality of natural laws, a kind of meta-causality. This implies that the choice of whether to act freely or not, is that of either acting in accordance with the essence of the causal principle, or in accordance with something derivative from it, like appetite. This would be easier to understand if it could be said that the phenomenal world was actually caused by the noumenal, in which free will is based, but Kant's narrowly

scientific definition of causality restricts causality wholly to the phenomenal side, which is thus deprived of any known connection with
the other. The Platonic idea of formal causality is ignored.

Kant will speak of actions proceeding from the noumenal subject, but not in him, again so as to be consistent with his conception
of the difference between the two realms. If causal action began in
the noumenal, it would be subject to temporal processes like those
of the empirical world, and so the distinction between them would
be lost. Consequently, he maintains that no change happens in the
noumenal subject, and so there is no cessation and no beginning-
to-be. This implies the possibility of full completeness or definitive
totality, which is by definition absent from the empirical world,
where all causal changes come about precisely through things newly
beginning to exist.

One consequence of this is that nothing in the world of phenomena can ever be an absolute beginning for any series of events, as
everything in it must by definition have an antecedent. A personal
consequence of this would be that our every action would have to
be referred back to something else as its origin, and that in turn to
something else, so that we could not properly be responsible for
anything. We then should be just transmitters of heteronomous
forces, and therefore without free will. But Kant's idea of the noumenal subject outside the chain of natural causality gives us the
entity from whence absolute beginnings can be made, even though
we cannot claim to know how it effects this. Reason is of the very
essence of this entity, and reason itself never changes in any way,
whence the variety of results it produces is owing only to the variety
of the situations to which it becomes related.

Should the subject be able to initiate new series of actions, there
need be no opposition to natural causality, thanks to the excess of
causal potential in the world, over possibilities for effects, according
to what was said previously. Another reason for there being no conflict between phenomenal and noumenal causality lies in the fact
that, for Kant, reason is the cause of the empirical laws to which our
natural inclinations are subject. Thus it appears that the essential
choice is between the rational cause operating directly, and its operating deviously and at second-hand through things which obscure

its true nature. But in either case, one and the same principle is at work, not two, and a purely delegated form of a power has no means of opposing the power itself when it acts without mediation.

Although the expressions are not used, the distinction made here is very close to that contained in the ideas of *natura naturans* and *natura naturata*, the former being a nature in some sense ontologically "before" the nature we ordinarily experience, as with the Platonic forms. As with Kant's distinction between noumena and phenomena, the relation between them is one-directional, as the one owes everything to the other, but not vice-versa. This kind of relation has been graphically expressed to the effect that: "nature (*natura naturata*) can, by human agency, invade reason (*natura naturans*) only to kill, whereas reason can invade nature to take prisoners and even colonize."[9]

Given this conception, the power of reason over nature is intrinsically unopposable, and the will which is assimilated to it is necessarily free, whereas the will becomes unfree as a result of a certain inversion of the natural causal priorities, whereby the derivative, *natura naturata*, is moved into a ruling place in the mentation of a being who belongs by nature to a causal plane above it. Reason thus combines in itself two properties which are apparently conflicting, those of causality and freedom. But freedom for Kant is not caprice, but determination by the highest form of causal power, although its function as cause goes beyond the phenomenal usage that Kant reserves for it, since it must be the cause behind natural causes.

Such is the conception of free will which would appear to allow the idea that our actions proceed in accordance with a causality that determinism would affirm, such that free will functions in parallel with external necessity, since Kant maintains that the course of phenomenal causes is not altered. But on the other hand, Kant also attributes real causal power to the free (rational) will, so it is clear that he does not give up the idea of the free will truly changing things, for all its harmonization with natural forces. The problem here is that of reconciling a flow of events containing no "first beginnings", but only "subordinate beginnings", with another one

9. C. S. Lewis, *Miracles*, chap. IV.

which does contain such beginnings. No solution to this problem is offered by Kant, but one answer to it is the conception of natural causality built up from broken sequences of causal processes, which I have premised previously. Causality in this form could be susceptible to outside agencies without losing its own nature.

In regard to the question of connecting the noumenal and phenomenal worlds, it is possible that Kant could be saying that the noumenon is unknowable mainly because of the fact that we cannot form any mental images of it. Nevertheless, there are in fact innumerable things we can understand without being able to imagine, though the fact does not seem to be referred to in this philosophy, as one might expect, if it had been given due consideration. Kant may have been misled by Hume's indiscriminate use of the word "ideas" both for mental conceptions and for mere sensory images. He has to admit that we know that the noumenal world exists, though it is not explained how we could know even that much, if it were as opaque to human knowledge as Kant maintains. Reason's highest function is said to be in distinguishing the sensible world from the intelligible or noumenal world, though this would hardly be possible if the most we knew of the latter was simply that something-or-other was there.

Whether intentionally or not, an important traditional idea of man as mediator between two worlds is being appealed to here. In its typical form[10] man knows himself to be the highest member of the natural order and the lowest member of the spiritual order, given that there is no theoretical objection to his knowledge of the latter. However, the effectiveness of this mediating function is clearly weakened in Kant's revival of the idea.

One problem of freedom which is addressed in the *Critique of Practical Reason* is that of reconciling the reality of freedom with its non-random functioning in accordance with law. Kant's predecessors had shown that we can know the moral law without our having any motive beyond the purely prudential, for obeying it. That would amount to a denial of its ontological primacy, a confession that it was in need of support extraneous to itself. Such a morality

10. See Aquinas, SCG., bk. ii, 68, (6).

would either have to contain an *a priori* element of self-interest, and so be practical but metaphysically impure, or else it would have to be composed of morally pure principles, while leaving us without any motive for acting in accordance with them.

Kant's answer to this is to show that the moral law is a direct product of man's use of his own reason, with the result that, by obeying it, he is simply obeying what is most essential to his own nature. On this basis, we have the answer to the question put by Lewis White Beck, "Can the human will be, at once spontaneous, obedient, and autonomous?"[11] Each of these three criteria will involve the others if Kant is right. It seems that the common sense alternatives of obedience either to external authority or to the inner light are now transcended, as also the alternatives of obeying impersonal principles or mere self-will. "[All] moral discipline is self-discipline, from which it follows that all just government is self-government."[12]

This idea of the relation between inner and outer authority has at least one antecedent in Scotus Eriugena, who maintained that reason is the first authority, and that all external forms of authority are simply reified forms of reason's own judgements.[13] If the outward is just the reification of the inward, there is no ultimate conflict, but this could only be perceived by rational beings who can discriminate the working of natural causes. From thence they learn the possibility of acting in accordance with the common principle of all causality, and not with particular instances of it.

This would be so if the will co-operated fully with the causal principle, but where it does not do so, external considerations have to be taken into account, such as one's relations with others, whence comes the idea of obligation, which supplies what is lacking to the moral will alone. Because our will is not perfectly good, there has to be the idea of duty, therefore. The Categorical Imperative relates only to what is good in itself, such as the performance of duty solely because reason shows it to be such. Only when it prevails, can the

11. *Studies in the Philosophy of* Kant, chap. XIII, III.
12. Ibid., p. 228.
13. *Periphyseon*, bk. I, 69.

actions in question properly be called free; any admixture from natural inclinations can only introduce determination and unfreedom.

Causal Origination

However, this issue still cannot be separated from the question of free will initiating new beginnings. We are given reason to adopt the interpretation of free will as objectively changing things where Kant speaks very disparagingly of the low profile view of it[14] which would equate it with the ability to do as one pleases, as this would leave us wholly in the web of causation. Such a freedom is spoken of in the same place as like the "freedom" of a turnspit to move after it has been wound up, something which the possession of consciousness could not alter, because a "thinking automaton" must be no less an automaton on that account.

He is concerned to deny that the noumenal basis of freedom has any involvement in time, as only the phenomenal world is subject to time. Nevertheless, he also speaks of man's "causality as a noumenon", whence there is the possibility of the idea of causation being enlarged to include extra-temporal reality. Thus everything about an unlawful action can be causally explained by its antecedents, but nevertheless both the action and its antecedents are all phenomena of the same noumenal personality. It would seem that this action, and the series of others related to it are all related to one another according to *efficient causality,* while the series as a whole is produced by the *formal causality* of the noumenon. Kant might well have used these Aristotelian terms to resolve the difficulty of using causality in regard to both phenomenal and noumenal-phenomenal relations, and the fact that he did not shows how much he was swayed by the intellectual fashions of his time.

A noumenon as formal cause would have to be knowable, however, though in a manner different from that of phenomena, but it could not be part of a causal system while being defined as unknowable. But knowable or not, Kant's system cannot work without a cause of this kind, and as guarantor of freedom, it might seem that

14. *Critique of Practical Reason,* pp. 190–191 Ak.V, 97.

determination by knowledge would detract from the freedom which the noumenal cause must itself possess primarily, but that would only deny it the freedom of arbitrariness, a freedom which Kant regards as unworthy of the name. The freedom of this kind of cause could be compromised by mutual relations of efficient causality between it and the phenomenal world, and as that is the only kind of relation considered by Kant, the relation between them is left completely unspecified. That our sensible nature is related to the "supersensible substratum in us," would seem to be as far as he could go in this regard.

In the same connection, we have Kant's denial[15] that God creates appearances or phenomena, rather in the manner in which Plato, for his own reasons, asserts[16] that the Demiurge creates only spiritual beings, including the Gods and rational souls, and that the creation of the material world is left to the latter. As God does not create phenomena as such, he cannot be said to be the creator of the interactions between them either. If, then, only the rational agents or noumena are divinely created, the unlawful and unfree acts of the will which occur in the phenomenal world could not be attributed to God.

As regards the relation of noumenon to phenomenon, there is still another aspect of the Kantian idea of causality which could be relevant. Causality is a Category, that is, it is not derived from experience, but rather makes our experience what it is. Given this conception, there does not seem to be much reason for confining it rigidly to the sensory world. Being an innate concept, it must, like everything else, manifest the thing-in-itself, though on a higher level. However, Kant seems not to wish to use this distinction, and rather places all knowables on the same level, whether they are conceptual or sensory.

Man is taken to be by definition a member of two worlds, the sensible and the intelligible at once, wherein he is determined as a phenomenon, and free as a noumenon. According to Lewis White Beck, "the initiation of a new series cannot be interpreted as an

---

15. *Critique of Practical Reason*, p. 196 Ak.V, 102.
16. *Timaeus*, 41a–d.

influxus mysticus without surrendering the category of causality."[17] Here, we can see that this commentator is simply taking for granted the all-or-nothing view of natural causality adopted by Kant. The reasons why this concession to determinism does not have to be made have been given.

There is no question of the *influxus mysticus* of the noumenon having to irrupt into a causal continuum. Nature can equally well be a structure of gaps, holes, and interstices, albeit permeated and connected by various uniform causal operations of finite lengths. This also means that there is no necessity to believe the notion that no one event could be made different without making the whole natural order different, which would seem to be merely a form of dogmatism. In this case, we should have the right to take Kant at his word in the passages where he speaks of free will as initiating new causal series.

Such a view could be held while accepting the principle that actions whose motives can be traced to external factors fall under natural causality, and so are not free, no matter how identified with them we may be. The only motive which comes exclusively from within us is the rational conviction that a given action is morally right and a duty, and if we act in accordance with that, we are acting freely. As freedom is both rational agency and the absence of phenomenal constraints, we are not aware of it directly, owing to this lack of phenomenal content. It is our knowledge of moral principles which makes us aware of it, together with our realization that we can act in accordance with them.

Free will belongs to all rational beings as such, and is exempt from the action of all natural causes, which does not mean that it is lawless. A lawless free will would be randomness, which would deprive it of meaning, because the idea of freedom is inseparable from the idea of purpose. Consequently, it must operate according to a law of which it itself is the author, which is the one way in which being subject to a law cannot mean being subject to a constraint. The criterion of lawfulness is universality, whence is derived the Categorical Imperative, that one must act in such a way that the action could be an application of a universal law.

17. *Studies in the Philosophy of Kant*, chap. 1, p. 37.

Appendix: Kant and Free Will

Only by acting in accordance with this principle is it possible for different individuals to will the same thing in a way which is more than merely conventional or simply libidinal. When people cannot will harmoniously, man-made regulations have to be imposed, thus suppressing freedom. The alternatives of being motivated either by practical reason or natural inclination do not imply an ultimate dualism because, in the *Groundwork,* it is stated that "the world of understanding contains the foundation of the world of sense." Although Kant revised this view in his later works, I think we should have the right to give due weight to it in view of the conception of causality on which the present study is based. We do not have to follow Kant in equating causality with its narrowly scientific form as efficient causality.

This means that the will's moral conflicts are between its being determined either by the world of understanding, or by impulses from the sense world, which is itself produced as a whole by the world of understanding. We thus have a choice of being governed by a cause in which we also share as co-causes, or of being governed by natural forces which act without regard to our supra-phenomenal nature, and which conflict with our possibility of sharing in the common ruling principle.

There is a definite similarity between these conceptions and Proclus' conception of freedom in his *Providence and Fate.* In this book, it is stated that Providence is prior to Fate, and that it produces "by a much greater priority" what is produced by Fate, but not vice-versa. Man is said to have the choice between being ruled by Providence or by Fate, the latter being caused *en bloc* by Providence without regard to individuals as such. The providential law has thus an intrinsic power over the fatal.[18] But in this philosophy the noumenal principle is knowable as the forms.

To return to the source of the Categorical Imperative, the main factor is that the moral laws which are imperative for each rational individual are also those of the understanding, because he personally participates in their source existentially. Conversely, the laws of nature or natural inclination cannot constitute an imperative for us

18. *Providence and Fate,* 3.

because, being physically necessary, they cannot form part of our noumenal self, the self with power of choice. Duties are therefore defined in relation to this as actions which conform to the laws of the understanding when seen as alternatives to actions based only on inclination. The option of duty has no power to compel one to adopt it, both because freedom is of its essence, and because that which really can compel belongs specifically to the realm of natural causation, to which duty is the alternative.

A Rational Idea of Happiness

Our participation in the noumenal source of phenomena, and therefore of their laws, makes us *a priori* able to discover and understand all laws of this kind. We have a natural and consubstantial insight into what lies behind appearances. This means that we can never actually admire unlawful actions in ourselves or in others, or practise them for their own sake, even though we may advise them for reasons of prudence. The idea of the lawful is always present to us as long as reason functions at all.

For these reasons, the basis of man's idea of his own worth lies in the degree of adequation of his will to the Categorical Imperative, and his corresponding freedom from natural causality. The moral law is the source of our knowledge of freedom, and not the other way round, as freedom is primarily a causality by reason which morality exemplifies. Practical reason cannot be derived from experience, as it is experience which depends on it. The causality with which the moral agent brings about his actions is thus of one and the same kind with the causality with which the Noumenon brings the phenomenal world into being.

We seem to have no reason to doubt that reason (as practical) is an efficient cause in the sense world, acting through ourselves as one class of its instruments. Kant speaks of the being with free will as a *causa noumenon*,[19] an idea which he claims is legitimate because unschematized causality derives from the understanding,

19. *Critique of Practical Reason*, pp. 145–146, Ak. V, 55.

182

not experience, whence it is "therefore not restricted to phenomena." This is also said to be an "empty" notion, because the noumenon by definition is not the subject of any experience which could provide examples. We can therefore know that free will is causal, but we cannot know what is involved in this. The problem here is solved for Platonism by the theory of the instancing of ideal-forms, and Kant shows an awareness of this possibility, where he says that the moral law proceeds from the *archetypal* world (*natura archetypa*), to the *ectypal* world (*nature ectypa*). The former is "a pure world of understanding whose counterpart must exist in the world of sense, but without interfering with its laws."[20] Nevertheless, this insight does not have the influence in his thinking which it should have had.

Elsewhere, he expresses a conception of freedom very much like the Plotinian-Augustinian idea of it, which makes it a determination by good, rather than an option:

> One might raise the objection that God cannot decide otherwise than he does, and so does not act freely, but out of the necessity of his nature. But man can always decide on something else . . . it is precisely this which is a lack of freedom in man. . . . Rather it is true freedom in God that he decides only what is suitable to his highest understanding.[21]

According to the *Critique of Practical Reason*, man can only be expected to participate in such a state after a length of development far in excess of a human lifetime, and which would therefore require him to have an immortal soul and live on in the hereafter. This development would culminate in the *Summum Bonum*, where the completeness of moral goodness and that of happiness coincide. Here again, Kant speaks within a tradition, as Gregory of Nyssa said that the truly perfect man was one who never became perfect because he was always becoming better. This reaching-forward was conceived to be endless, both here and in the hereafter, whereas Kant only implies that the process is very long, not infinite.

20. Ibid., p. 132.
21. *Lectures on Philosophical Theology*, Ak 43 'Physicotheology', pp. 104–106.

The pursuit of happiness in the sensory world cannot be freely willed because every state in this realm is either one or a small number of manifestations of its noumenal or formal Cause, and therefore bound to be succeeded by others which will not necessarily be prolongations of it. Therefore free will must be directed to the Cause, so as to aim at the cause of happiness, rather than the happiness which is only an effect in a limited time-span. The unfree will is a cause of unhappiness by reason of a mistaken attachment to the ephemeral which goes so far as to prevent any counter-attachment to its Cause.

Much of the importance of Kant's philosophy is owing to its being a revival of a significant part of the Great Tradition. The fact that he was not consciously attempting any such thing only emphasizes the paradigmatic nature of the intelligence, which tends to revert to the same principles of its own accord. As if aware that his presentation of the doctrine was far from complete, Kant's development of it in great detail could be taken as an unconscious compensating reaction. In the process of it, he derives a conception of free will which is very close to that of Platonism, as discussed already.

Index

Adam, J. 27
Agency 126–129, 138, 152
Alexander of Aphrodisias 60–81
Aquinas, St.Thomas 77, 176
Anthropic Principle 33, 151
Aristotle 6, 56, 60–63, 70, 73,
    79–82, 95, 99, 124, 145
Augustine, St. 36, 82, 84, 87–90,
    104, 155
Autonomy 15

Barrow, J.D. and Tipler, F.J. 33
Beck, Lewis White 177, 179–180
Boethius 67–68
Brain-scans 132–135
Buddhism 59

Calvinism 74
Catholicism 156–157
Causality, efficient 78, 81, 161, 178
Causality, formal 71, 81, 161, 178
Cause *per accidens* 64, 67, 69
Causes, natural 22, 77, 143, 149,
    165, 177, 180
Chance 17–18
Choice 48–50, 158–159
Christian thought 7–9, 16, 37, 55,
    59, 104, 135, 140, 158
Cicero 8
Civilization 12, 77–78
Coincidences 70–72
Commandments 52
Conjoint principle 55
Conversion 16

Cornford, F.M. 15, 19
Criteria
Cushman, R.E. 15–16

Deliberation 65–66, 99–100
Demiurge 17, 19, 21
Determinism 38–39, 67, 78, 81,
    83, 111, 130–132, 136, 140, 150
Dostoyevsky, F. 156
Dualism 10–11, 14, 54–55, 139, 153
Duty 120–122

Entropy 141, 143–144
Equality, social 11–12
Epinomis dialogue 85–86
Eros 16, 25
Ethics, Aristotle's 6, 56, 66, 79–
    80, 97
Evil 46, 52–53
Exemption, of soul 57

Fall, the 9
Fatalism 38, 78
Fate 68–69, 80–81, 162, 181
Findlay, J.N. 18, 71
First Cause 47, 61, 62
Free will, criteria of 43
Freedom, absolute 135
Freedom and the possible 46,
    102–103

Gnosticism 37–38
God 27, 54, 73–75, 86–87, 94,
    122, 135, 140, 149, 155, 164, 183

Good, the 18, 44, 93
Gordian III, Emperor 35
Gospels 53
Guilt, absolute 104

Happiness 120
Harris, Victor 73
Hume, David 39, 67, 105, 107–
109, 170–171, 176

Iamblichus 9–10
Images, mental 138–140
Imperative, Categorical 125–126,
177, 181

Incas, the 157
Indifference, liberty of 108–109,
112–113, 178–179
Individualism 157
Intellect, human 58–59
Intellectual-principle 41–42, 54,
65, 73
Intelligence 42, 135–138
Intelligibles, the 32

Jung, C.G. 106

Kant, Immanuel 4, 7, 14, 21, 61,
114–115, 119–126, 151, 159, 163–
184
Koestler, Arthur 129

Laws, Plato's 94–97, 99, 100
Lethe 28
Lewis, C.S. 153, 175
Linguistic philosophy 127
Lovejoy, A.O. 53, 139

Macrocosm 28, 49, 157
Material world 43, 161–162
Maturation 106–107

Metaphysical realities 34, 44
Metaphysics, Aristotle's 7, 70
Microcosm 23, 34, 43, 49, 58, 152,
157
Minds, objectively real 127–129
Monism 2

Narcissus, myth of 93
Nature 68–69, 73, 175
Necessity 3, 14–15, 17–18, 20, 31,
107
Neoplatonism 36, 58, 138–140
New Testament 155

Oedipus 40, 43
Old Testament 52
Omnipotence 19
Order, universal 57

Passions 116–119
Phaedrus dialogue 32, 87, 88
Philo of Alexandria 36
Pieper, Joseph 172
Plato 14–34
Platonism 150–152, 172, 183, 184
Plotinus 35–59
Popper, Karl 132
Power, causal 24
"Privation" 64, 73, 100, 148
Proclus 2, 35, 36, 111, 115, 149, 152,
181
Providence 51–52
Pythagoras 17

Reason, objective 19, 20, 24, 33,
68, 160, 175
Reformation, the 75
Regress, infinite 50–51, 115, 167
Reincarnation 44, 50
Religion and free will 1, 75, 155,
156

Index

Republic Book X 16, 28, 30–31, 44, 54, 85
Ross, Sir David 120, 121

Salvation 55
Self-determination 16
Self-motion 24–26, 146–147
Self-verification 12–13
Series, causal 32, 45, 174, 180
Shafarevitch, Igor 157
Sin, original 54
Socrates 17
Sophist dialogue 63
Sorabji, Richard 69
Soul 5, 21, 23, 28, 33, 40–42, 54–55, 86, 89, 145–148
Soviet Union 158
Stars 47

Statesman dialogue 27
Stoics 60, 81
Synchronicity 48

Tao Te Ching 58
Technology 15
Thermodynamics, Second Law of 28, 145
Timaeus dialogue 4, 14, 17, 20, 27, 32, 37, 51, 54, 83, 143

Uncaused causality 62, 64, 69, 164
Universe 14

Wallis, R. T. 46
Wilhelm, Richard 91
World Soul 5, 23, 25